Holy virility

Emmanuel Reynaud

Holy virility
*The social construction
of masculinity*

translated by Ros Schwartz

Pluto Press

First published in France in 1981 as *La Sainte
Virilité* by Editions Syros, 9 Rue Borromée – 75015
Paris

Copyright © Editions Syros 1981

Translation first published in 1983 by Pluto Press
Limited, The Works, 105a Torriano Avenue
London NW5 2RX

Translation copyright © Pluto Press 1983

ISBN 0-86104-399-5

Computerset by Promenade Graphics Limited
Unit 23a Lansdown Industrial Estate
Cheltenham, Gloucestershire
Printed in Great Britain by St Edmundsbury Press
Bury St Edmunds, Suffolk IP33 3TU

Contents

1. Introduction

Old ideas die hard; in spite of our increasingly precise understanding of the mechanisms of oppression, the division of humanity into men and women is still generally presented as natural. The fact that throughout history 'nature' has always been invoked to justify the power of one group over another has not, for most people, cast any doubt over the validity of the division of humankind into sexes. People who assert that the mother's presence is essential to a child's development during the first eighteen months, or that childbearing is woman's greatest fulfilment, are disguising what is cultural by claiming that it is natural. The same attitude is found in people who argue that it was natural for black people to be slaves on the cotton plantations as the pigmentation of their skin protected them from the sun's rays. When physical characteristics like black people's skin pigmentation or women's aptitude for pregnancy are used as arguments to subject the former to cultivating cotton and the latter to rearing children, then it is no longer a question of nature but, quite simply, of oppression. Cotton-picking or childcare are not prescribed by biology, they are imposed by a social relation of power in which one group exploits another and tries to camouflage its exploitation with naturalist or biologising explanations.

The argument for a natural difference between the sexes has been disproved by a whole series of discoveries. We now know, particularly from Margaret Mead's work,[1] that psychological characteristics, behaviour and social roles traditionally attributed to one or the other sex in the West vary considerably according to different societies and are often even reversed. Among the Chambuli in New Guinea, to mention but one example, to be level-headed is considered typically feminine:

the women are the dominant partners and the men are considered less able and more emotional. Similarly, anatomical distinctions associated with physical strength, supposed to be an irremediable factor in dividing the sexes, appear to be considered differently in different places. In a number of cultures men and women are of the same height and build and in some societies the men are even smaller and less sturdy than the women. Robert Briffault[2] cites the African Ashiras and Bashalingas as well as the Bushmen where the women are on average 4cms taller than the men. Moreover, if we go back in history and consider our Paleolithic ancestors, studies of the earliest human remains have revealed that there was a very slight difference in height between men and women, and that their bones were of almost identical diameter.

In a more general work, Pierre Samuel[3] gives a number of examples, historical and contemporary, where women are as strong as, or stronger than, men. He has found numerous women pirates, outlaws, warriors and fighters who had been ignored by official history; societies in which the women hunt or make war, with or without the men; others in which boxing matches are mixed; others where pregnancy does not prevent women from continuing their usual activities, which are only briefly interrupted while they give birth.

To add to the list of examples of societies where there is little dimorphism or where the male and female attributes and roles are inversed would not make it any more convincing. It is not necessary to gather proof of the contradictory character of the supposedly natural sexual differences, to remind ourselves of the too frequently forgotten fact concerning man and woman, which is that humans do not exist in a natural state, outside social relationships, but that they are precisely a product of those relationships.

The division into sexes

One of the reasons for the confusion that reigns whenever the division into sexes is discussed is the amalgam made between the differences which are in fact natural, and those resulting from a social structure where men and women form two distinct groups. What can be said about natural differences? Only that they are related to the sexed mode of reproduction; the aptitude for reproduction does not depend on the individual but on the species. Like all the living beings which reproduce by interbreeding, humans have a male and a female variant.

The mechanism of sexual differentiation is fairly well known; it begins at conception, according to whether the pair of sexual chromosomes consists of XX or XY; this genetic sex causes a hormonal process which determines the development of the sexual organs; in the end it is the external appearance of the physical organs which determines the legal sex at birth.

Thus there are two sexual differentiations: one is biological (genetical, hormonal and physical), and makes a person either male or female; the other is social, and is based solely on the appearance of the external sexual organs. It determines whether a person belongs to the group of men or to the group of women. The social gender may well not correspond to the biological gender. As a result of mistaken diagnosis in the event of genital anomaly, for example, a legal gender may be attributed to a child which might be unrelated to its biological sex. Robert Stoller[4] reports a large number of such errors. The study of these cases reveals how important upbringing can be in irrevocably determining sexual identity. Attempts to rectify the 'mistaken' identification and to restore the 'correct' one in accordance with the biological gender can even prove traumatic. Stoller cites the case of a girl who became psychotic when she was told, at the age of 14, that she was 'neuter', or 'perhaps a man'. These errors are, of course, relatively rare, however they emphasise the arbitrariness of a social decision which imposes two different behaviour patterns, depending on whether one has a vulva or a penis.

Instead of acknowledging that the fundamental biological differences between men and women are limited to the different functions of the male and female organs in reproduction, certain scientists attempt, on the contrary, to extend them to the behaviour and aptitudes of each sex.

Much research is based on the discovery that the nervous

structures of the foetus are impregnated with sexual hormones which determine the function of the hypothalamus; whether it will be stable and produce male hormones, or cyclical, and produce the two types of female hormones. From this better understanding of the mechanism of biological sexual differentiation numerous experiments have been carried out – on animals – relating human behaviour to hormones. Other studies along the same lines attempt to show that because the cerebral hemispheres are supposed to develop and function differently in men and women, aptitudes vary according to sex: women have superior verbal faculties, and men deal with global situations better than women.

This kind of research, which attempts to give a biological justification to socially determined sexes, needs comment. Actually, although it takes into account the influence of 'psychosocial factors' on biological behavioural determinism in the formation of the individual, it seems to ignore the fact that biological factors themselves are not static but are the product of a relationship to the environment, as much in the case of the individual (ontogenesis) as in the history of the species (phylogenesis). Thus, men and women as they are today, have nothing to do with any kind of 'human nature', nor with 'male and female natures', but are the product of the social division into two antagonistic sexes. What is the point of seeking to define the aptitudes and potential of each sex, when it is impossible at present for individuals to discover and develop their own potential precisely because they are confined within sex categories?

The urge to attribute the social differentiation between the sexes to biological causes is, first and foremost, a political stance. All these studies which are generally presented as a step towards 'understanding non-conformity' (or, 'homosexuality explained by hormones' . . .) and as a path towards equality between men and women through the development of the specificities of each sex, are in fact the expression of a different project: maintaining the status quo with a few rearrangements necessary to make it more palatable. Raoul Vaneigem[5] would call it simply: 'humanising the inhuman'. The attitude of these scientists is to consider that the present situation is definitive;

and that it more or less corresponds to the biological limits of human evolution. Therefore it is not for them to question the norms and categories in force, but only to alleviate their malfunction. Faced with individuals rebelling against their confinement within a category, they do not dispute the validity of that category, they attempt to protect it and put down the revolt. What does the individual matter, in other words, providing each person takes his or her allotted place . . . paving the way for a Brave New World?

However, arguments based on biology could take us in a totally different direction. The very specificity of the sexed mode of reproduction is that it creates a new being. The matching of two genetic programmes produces a new programme which is unlike others, unique of its kind. Recent biochemical findings even invalidate the concept of race or sub-species. The differences, not only among humans, but also among animals, would seem to be much greater than was hitherto supposed. François Jacob, the biologist,[6] cites the example of a certain species of snail found in North America, of which zoologists recognised 68 sub-species ten years ago, whereas today there are nearly 680 known sub-species. He adds, criticising the concept of race and the classification of the species in sub-species, 'there could almost be a race for each individual'. If we are going to be particular about differences, why stop at one rather than another? Why not go all the way, and realise that they are so numerous, that it is impossible to speak of categories – man or woman, black or white, short or tall – but only of individuals so diverse that none can be classified.

What does it matter to me, finally, to know whether or not I share a better perception of space with the other males of the species: I know that mine has nothing in common with that of theirs, as it has been shaped by my own experience, which I share with nobody.

Whatever the biological differences between males and females may be, they should not mask the fact that the division into men and women is purely social. From the minute a child is born, it is assigned to a sex category, according to its possessing a penis or a vulva. A person's entire identity develops on the basis of this sexual differentiation and through identification within that category; to such an extent that what has been imposed eventually seems natural. The category is so well assimilated that to question it would be to run the risk of being confronted with a vacuum – 'If I am not a man, what am I? Who am I?' And so when it is a question of 'male' and 'female' roles, we are not dealing with a role played here and there in such and such a situation, but with a real shell which the person has completely adopted, and which has been gradually built up during an existence governed by the differences between the sexes.

This division of human beings into two groups depending on their anatomy has been radically questioned by the feminist movement. Following Simone de Beauvoir's 'One is not born, but rather becomes, a woman',[7] the radical feminists have been determined to destroy the notion of the sex difference and attack the naturalist ideology, according to which, for instance, women are freely placed at men's disposal, not because they are appropriated by men, but because passivity, washing up and tenderness are specifically 'feminine' characteristics. They have shown that the concepts of 'woman' and 'man' are the justification and the result of a relationship of oppression, and only when these concepts have been eliminated will it be possible for each person to develop her or his potential as an individual.

Men's reactions to this clarification have not varied much. Even today they oscillate mainly between varied attempts by the majority to salvage their threatened power, and feelings of guilt among a minority for belonging to the oppressive sex; but those who agree to question the idea of being a 'man' are few and far between. Obviously a person who wields power and a person who endures it do not share the same perceptions of reality. For a woman, being confined within a sex category is all the more sharply felt to be a form of mutilation for it corresponds directly with her oppression: 'to kill the myth of the "woman", including its most seductive aspects',[8] for women, means to get rid of an ideological structure which denies their identity as individuals and justifies their exploitation. For men, on the contrary, their category symbolises their power; and everything which defines them as 'masculine' is valorising, even to the extent that men do not generally see themselves as a separate group, but rather as a reference for the species – are not humans as a rule referred to as 'man'?

Why should a man question the category 'man'? The question could be rephrased. Why should a man want to give up all the material, psychological and emotional advantages that he enjoys as a result of the division into sexes? Why would an oppressor give up his dominant position of his own free will?

Of course, recently, since the appearance of the women's liberation movement, this position has become less stable: male prerogatives are not as solid as they were before. Christine Delphy[9] describes it as the change in perspective 'which separates the "I'm not a feminist but . . . " of the pre-seventies and the "I'm not a chauvinist but . . . " of the eighties.' In homes, factories and offices affected by feminist ideas – and there are more and more of them – men actually have to stall and justify obtaining what was previously their 'natural' due. The arguments are multifarious: from the 'You're not mistaken but I'm too old to change now' to 'I would iron my shirts but I was never taught to iron' or 'Honestly! Why do you always belittle yourself? Isn't it wonderful to be a good cook; isn't it as important as building nuclear power stations?' The tone varies but a man sometimes has to use his imagination if he wants to continue being waited on hand and foot. What was formerly taken for granted – shopping, cooking, housework, production and rearing of children, conjugal rights, love, admiration, tenderness, etc. – give rise more and more frequently to conflicts and compromises.

Whatever the discomfort this new state of affairs causes men would doubtless be of little importance if men–women relationships could be reduced to the sum of individual relationships. But one of the achievements of the feminist movement is to have shown that the antagonism between the sexes, far from being limited to conflicts between isolated individuals, is part of a well-defined social structure – patriarchy. Thus the categories 'man' and 'woman' are not simply entities which could be tinkered with in order to solve the problem of oppression; they are the product and the instrument of patriarchal power. And if the question of why a man should question his category does not have an obvious answer, we can ask another question first: what does being a 'man' within patriarchy mean?

The origins of patriarchy

Patriarchy generally succeeds in deceiving people; even though our daily lives are governed by it, many people only see it in distant lands or remote periods of history. The forms through which it is articulated today, private or state capitalism, can disguise its own mechanisms of oppression and exploitation. But whatever the particular modes of production it secretes, patriarchy is characterised first and foremost by the division of humans into sexes, which is expressed by the appropriation of women and the struggle for power among men.

The development of patriarchy has been almost universal, which makes it difficult, today, to trace its origins. In spite of carbon dating, pollen analysis, the study of age-rings on wooden tools, the discovery of bones, jewellery and various objects and instruments, the progress of anthropology, ethology and linguistics, we still know almost nothing of the origins of patriarchy and what human relations could have been like before it existed. In the last hundred years or so there have been numerous attempts to reconstruct the past: from Bachofen's[10] theory of matriarchy and his 'Mother Rights' to the recent hypothesis about 'matriarchal societies in the old world' by Ernest Borneman,[11] there are many scenarios. Yet the pre-patriarchal period is still a mystery and looks as though it will remain one for a long time to come.

Why are human beings separated into two groups? Why and how have men taken a dominant position? It would no doubt be interesting to be able to answer these questions; many people have tried recently, but the dire shortage of tangible information encourages them to give free rein to their fantasies. Instead of admitting their ignorance of the 'origin', as soon as the subject of male–female relationships is raised everybody takes advantage of the opportunity to invent a history of the beginning. The fantasies include fear of castration, penis envy, vagina envy, desire to give birth, a fire jealously guarded by women against the threat of masculine urine, a corral of pregnant women who wait for the men hunters to return, etc. Formed by projections of present conditions into the past, such fantasies would be of little consequence if it were not for the fact that they are used to construct a justification of the present.

When one is not concerned with maintaining patriarchy but with destroying it, what is the point of inventing an 'origin'? To what extent can the reconstruction of a long-forgotten past contribute to our understanding of the present situation? Is it really necessary to know how power came about in order to convince ourselves that it is unjustifiable?

Although we cannot satisfy our curiosity about the origin of patriarchy, we can still study the ideological description of it with some hopes of understanding its modern forms. It is not feasible here to study all the myths of the different patriarchal cultures; I shall confine myself to the one which concerns us most directly: Judeo–Christian civilisation. The genesis and basis of its ideology have the advantage of being easily accessible, thanks to the opening pages of the Old Testament. Naturally we do not find any explanation of the hierarchical division of human beings into sexes, because the ABC of any patriarchal ideology is precisely to present that division as being of biological, natural or divine essence. On the other hand, we can get a clear picture of patriarchal logic which, from the division of the sexes, develops into the appropriation of women and the struggle for power among men. The distinctive feature of the Old Testament account of the Creation is that it divides into two separate narratives which offer contradictory versions of the creation of human beings. They do not always appear as such because of the mechanisms of patriarchal thinking and deceptive language, where to be human and to be a man are considered one and the same thing; but nevertheless they are divergent.

The first version presents the creation of a human being which could just as easily be male as female: 'So God created man in his own image; in the image of God he created him; male and female he created them.' (*Genesis* I:27; all quotations from the Bible are taken from the New English Bible, 1970.) Some commentators have interpreted this to mean that the 'first' human being was androgynous, but the plural pronoun in 'He created *them*' dispels any confusion: it is certainly about human beings as they actually are, that is, comprising a male sex and a female sex. The god himself is in their image and has nothing to do with a Father-Creator. However, if the differentiation according to sex criteria does not imply any hierarchy here, it is still made, and points to what is to follow. Indeed, why differentiate if it is not to form a hierarchy?

The second version states matters clearly. Delivered by a different narrator, it consists of a fresh account: this time the 'first' human being is created from 'the dust of the ground' (II:7) and, as we discover a few verses later, is no longer made up of a male and female; now *he* is alone. 'Then the Lord God said: It is not good for the man to be alone. I will provide a partner for him.' (II:18) This description attempts to suggest a poor male lost in the wilderness without his traditional submissive and devoted companion. But if we do not allow the author to bamboozle us but follow the text, we see that this first 'man' is neither man nor woman, 'he' represents the human being not divided into sexes. Moreover, the allusion to the absence of a partner leads up to the need for this division which is soon presented quite specifically:

> And so the Lord God put the man into a trance, and while he slept, he took one of his ribs and closed the flesh over the place. The Lord God then built up the rib, which he had taken out of the man, into a woman. He brought her to the man and said: 'Now this at last—bone from my bones, flesh from my flesh!—this should be called woman, for from man was this taken.' (II:21–23)

This creation could appear at first to be only that of 'woman'; but on closer examination, reading between the lines, it is also the creation of 'man'. In fact, the way the separation is described, if the woman is only a 'rib' of a human, man himself is only a human missing a 'rib'.

This new understanding of the text sheds a different light on the division of the sexes. The creation of 'man' and of 'woman' appears to be the result of an unequal but complementary mutilation of the human being depending on his or her sex: minus a 'rib' for one of them, minus everything except a 'rib' for the other. The individual with either the smaller or greater part of him or herself thus amputated, is subsequently supposed to retrieve his or her integrity thanks to complementarity: 'That is why a man leaves his father and mother and is united to his wife, and the two become one flesh'. (II:24) The text comes the full circle: man severs a part of himself which he calls 'woman', and then appropriates a woman to reconstitute, in the couple, the mutilated human being. Having created the sex categories and begun to define them, all that is left is for the narrator to finish off his work with a striking myth: original sin.

The story is very well known but is generally taken at face value, without being examined critically. Yet the scene depicts the archetypal heterosexual patriarchal relationship. Man, who is already minus a 'rib', is parted from his sexuality, symbolised by a snake. With the help of deception – call it smooth talk – and with the phallus snake as go-between, 'More crafty than any wild creature that the Lord God had made' (III:1) man seduces woman and together they discover 'good and evil'. This odd way of making love in a threesome, the phallus, the woman and the man, which is presented as the first sexual relationship, is in reality the standard heterosexual relationship and is institutionalised as such:

> Then the Lord God said to the snake: 'Because you have done this you are accursed more than all cattle and all wild creatures. On your belly you shall crawl, and dust you shall eat all the days of your life.' (III–14)

Male sexuality, confined to the penis, is reduced to less than nothing—and that is not all:

> I will put enmity between you and the woman between your brood and hers. They shall strike at your head and you shall strike at their heel. (III:15)

If we bear in mind the fact that, in the Bible, 'foot' is often used as a euphemism for sexual organ, we can imagine what the woman's 'heel' represents . . . the image of the head of the penis crushing the vulva on its way into the vagina plainly evokes the heterosexual relationship within patriarchy. And it is once this type of relationship is institutionalised that the creation of the categories 'man' and 'woman' becomes complete.

> To the woman he said 'I will increase your labour and
> your groaning and in labour you will bear children. You
> shall be eager for your husband and he shall be your
> master.' (III:16)

Not one word is superfluous in the definition of the life of woman: suffering, giving birth often and in pain, and an irresistible 'desire' to be dominated by a man. As for man, he, apart from the fact that he dominates a woman, is definitely identified with the human species, and his life is presented as a daily struggle:

> And to the man he said: 'because you have listened to
> your wife and have eaten from the tree which I forbade
> you, accursed shall be the ground on your account. With
> labour you shall win your food from it all the days of your
> life. It will grow thorns and thistles for you—none but
> wild plants for you to eat. You shall gain your bread
> by the sweat of your brow until you return to the ground;
> for from it you were taken. Dust you are, to dust you shall
> return.' (III:17–19)

After this long account of the life of 'man', the allusion to returning to dust completes his identification with the human being who was created from that same dust, but who was not yet a 'man' because he still had all his 'ribs'. This final sleight of hand endeavours to make us forget that the creation of 'man' was that of a mutilated human being, missing a part of itself, called 'woman', and whose sexuality is limited to an external phallus/snake. In spite of this final attempt to conceal the reality of the myth, it is nevertheless apparent that it is through his own mutilation that man establishes his domination over woman.

Mutilation as foundation

This division of the human being into 'man' and 'woman' by the unequal mutilation of the individual depending on the anatomy of the sexual organs is the basis on which the entire Judeo-Christian ideology is built. The Bible itself, once the sex categories have been defined through the myth of original sin, hardly does more than illustrate how they work. And so, from the next verse of the following chapter, man immediately uses 'his' wife so that she can carry out her allotted task without delay and bear children: 'She conceived and gave birth to Cain. She said "With the help of the Lord I have brought a man into being". Later she had another child, his brother Abel. Abel was a shepherd and Cain a tiller of the soil.' (IV:1–2) And these first sons of 'man' see their life so much as a struggle that after Abel's clear victory, 'Cain attacked his brother Abel and murdered him.' (IV:8) The fight to the death between men for power begins with the myth of the farmer who eliminates the shepherd – an historical short-cut which alludes to a conflict between sedentariness associated with agriculture and the nomadic existence of stock farming.

Cain the farmer, still gloating over his final success, leaves the country, under the protection of his god, and builds a town to establish his newly increased share of power. He had, naturally, appropriated a woman who would bear him the inevitable child: 'Cain was then building a city, which he named Enoch after his son.' (IV:17) After the construction of this first city the narrator considers the Judeo-Christian patriarchy definitively inaugurated. The biblical account abandons the mythical sphere and imperceptibly draws closer to reality, describing, through the wanderings of the Hebrews, struggles which Man takes up in the name of that entity symbolic of power, God. This competition for power and glory is to bring with it a real tide of tears and blood to be handed down from father to son. The Bible spares us no detail, right up to the apotheosis of the crucifixion of the son of 'man' for the glory of the Father.

Judeo-Christian ideology has become more sophisticated since its beginnings in the Old Testament. Through its various transformations, it has served as a foundation for the most powerful form of patriarchy, which now threatens to destroy the world in its struggle for hegemony. Judeo-Christian patriarchy is so highly developed that it finds itself confronting the antagonism born from the very origin of patriarchal organisation: the division of humans into sexes, or, in other words, the division of society into sex classes.

The bourgeoisie broke the old religious order which upheld the power of the feudal lords, and developed their own power by developing the productive forces. This process set in motion forces which threaten the basis of Judeo-Christian patriarchy – all the contradictions that spring from the appropriation of the woman class, and the power struggle within the man class are coming to a head. As the economic crisis worsens and the risk of nuclear war increases, the last twenty years have brought, for the first time it seems, earnest attempts to answer the fundamental question that the reign of patriarchy raises for humanity: how can power be eliminated?

By the end of the sixties, it was clear, for some people, that 'The problem of the proletariat is no longer to take power, but to put an end to it once and for all.'[12] And a few years later the feminist movement forcefully reminded us that power 'is at the tip of the phallus'. It is not difficult to make the connection between the two: it is to be found in every one of us, biologically male and socially 'men'. It is of crucial importance that we grasp the situation, especially as there is not much time left to untangle history.

Whatever the truth about the origins of patriarchy, since it has been established, human history has been that of a fundamental division which has created and conditioned all the others: the social distinction between men and women. Today, now that it is so highly developed that we have been brought face to face with the question of its origin, it is not a matter of reinforcing the sex division, but of abolishing it: of unmasking images which disguise power relations. Reappraising an underestimated 'femininity' and reassessing a wrongly evaluated 'virility' will not make any difference to oppression: our lives are not governed by values which each one of us can modify as we please to escape the oppressive reality; they are ruled by ideologies, institutions and modes of production which patriarchy secretes all over the globe.

When it comes to abolishing patriarchy the problem for men is not for them to create a 'new man', but, on the contrary, to destroy that 'man' from whom, as males, we have *all* been created, and who, in one way or another, we have *all* reproduced. It is to that process of destruction that I hope to contribute by describing men's attitudes to their body, their penis, sexuality and relationships with women and other men.

As for the question which worries some men – knowing what a male who is not a 'man' could be: each man can discover that for himself in a variety of pleasures available when one is relieved of the burden of fitting into a category. It would, however, be an act of deception to divorce this issue from the fact that as men within patriarchy we are, whether we want it or not, the embodiment of power.

2. Man and his body

In his race for power, man is able to separate mind and body: he sees the mind as transcending the human condition, and he turns his body into the place of natural alienation. He does not generally acknowledge that his body takes any part in thought, 'an activity of the brain as walking is an activity of the legs',[1] he most frequently perceives it as a faculty distinct from the body. He sees his body as a mere support for the mind, a support which can be cumbersome given the material contingencies it depends on: 'For the body causes us a thousand problems through the need for us to feed it; what is more it is subject to illness, and we are hindered in our search for reality. It fills us with loves, desires, fears, all kinds of fancies, innumerable stupidities to the extent that it makes it totally impossible for us to think.' (Plato)

The separation of mind and body is illustrated by the primacy of the mind and the sacrifice of the body. It is the base on which philosophers have 'interpreted the world' and, in the last analysis, it is on this premise that they have attempted to 'change' it; but, on a more general level, the way man relates to his body revolves round this dichotomy. In fact, whatever his approach, from the training of the sportsman who seeks to endure suffering, to the sophisticated techniques of the monk who forces himself to withdraw from his flesh, the ultimate aim is invariably the same: to dominate the body in the hope of being free of it. Religion is doubtless the most extreme expression of this attitude; all man's dreams and aspirations are united in the desire to create a disembodied entity, a pure mind, a god. Christianity even brings off a *tour de force* in personifying its god, and then doing away with his body in full view of everybody. This blood-soaked body, nailed to the cross, is moreover such an apt symbol of the body sacrificed by man in his race for power that it is the image on which present day Judeo-Christian patriarchy has been built.

The disappearing body

Man reproduces the body/mind separation that he creates in himself in his relationships with women. Just as he tends to picture himself as pure mind, so he sees woman as unrestrained flesh, a body over which the head has no control. He likes to consider himself a cultural being, almost completely free of natural contingencies, while he represents woman as a sort of natural being still subject to the obscure forces of nature. On this basis he defines as 'masculine', not only the few characteristics associated with the male sex, but all the human traits in which he acknowledges an ability to combat natural alienation. In the same way, he calls 'feminine' all those characteristics which submit to that alienation. Thus he makes woman into the symbol of his own dependence, and in addition, the further he dissociates himself from her, the more he feels he is his own master; he creates two definitions, femininity and virility, which exacerbate the anatomical differences, increase women's dependence and concentrate everything that seems to represent human strength in himself.

Man seeks to rid himself of the 'rib' which he parts with symbolically: while he cultivates all that he defines as 'virile', he does his best to reject what he calls 'feminine'. He wants to be strength, rationality and transcendence, whereas woman is weakness, irrationality and immanence. At one fell swoop he imposes 'femininity' on woman and is determined for his part, to be virile, and to differentiate himself clearly from her. He searches out and prizes the slightest details which distinguish males from females; so, body-hair, beard and penis become images of strength and symbols of power.

As for penis and testicles, they are the very criteria on which belonging to the man class depends. They assume paramount importance. Body-hair and beard denote virility and its first appearance. In adolescence man rushes to buy a razor; until he has ravaged his face with its blade, he is not really a man. As soon as a light down appears he starts to shave, especially as it is well known that the more hairs are cut, the faster and thicker they grow. To be beardless is no trifle – it evokes the innocence of childhood, or even worse, femininity. Of uncertain virility, a man without a beard is therefore not to be trusted. Furthermore, it is an insult which always has its adherents; Juan Perón, a short time before his death, jeered: 'beardless, mercenary idiots'.

But the beard is not sufficient; to be a man you must sport the insignia of power on your arms, legs, armpits and pubis as early as possible. Beach, swimming pool and shower can thus become such a nightmare for the adolescent whose virginal skin is still hairless that he often helps nature along in the privacy of the bathroom, exchanging with his friends the most extraordinary recipes to speed up the growth of hair. As he gets older, he does not necessarily outgrow his obsession with hairiness; he may very well have problems with a smooth chest or sparse growth on his arms or legs, and it is not unusual to find advertisements in the press promising abundant hair or offering a varied choice of sideburns and false moustaches.

However, man is not only preoccupied with being hairy, he also takes an interest in his muscles and his brain; he sees the strength of the human being in them and sees them as typically masculine organs. Unlike the penis, and, to a lesser degree, body-hair and beard, they are present in both the male and female. Man must therefore, in order to make them into criteria of differentiation, favour them in the male, and do his best to discount them in the female. Whilst he sees himself as strong and rational, woman should be fragile and irrational; and whereas he considers himself capable of thinking and transforming the world, he likes to imagine that she is hardly capable of coping.

And when, in spite of everything, a woman comes out with an indisputably pertinent statement, it is not because of the activity of her brain, but because of her renowned 'feminine intuition': women are not supposed to know how to think logically. When, during fairground challenges, women fighters start to get the better of their male opponents, mixed matches are forbidden, because women are not supposed to know how to fight.

This attitude has a twofold advantage for man: it deepens the rift between the sexes, enhancing his own physical and mental abilities to face the world, whilst it restricts those of the woman. This way he establishes his power so firmly that he ends up presenting it as 'natural'. Indeed, why shouldn't he dominate since he is the strongest and the most intelligent?

Whereas woman is supposed to be flesh with neither brain nor muscle, man interprets the body/mind dichotomy by seeing himself as a head which commands his muscles. He makes his body the instrument of his power by setting greater store on his cerebral and muscular activities; and he attaches more or less importance to the one or the other depending on his hierarchical position within the man class. Whereas the mind always controls the body, body and mind do not always belong to the same man.

In the same way that the dead god on the cross is the son of the Father, the strong arm of power, the body which is physically sacrificed to serve any entity whatever – glory, honour, freedom – is generally dissociated as far as possible from the brain which is really in control. Thus when man gives orders to bomber pilots from the depths of the presidential office, he is not usually worried about his muscles: his head alone is sufficient to guarantee his power, and the rest of his body becomes merely a receptacle for his brain. The advantage of this position is, other than the power it reflects, that it enables him, on the one hand, to avoid assault and battery, and, on the other, not to be dependent on the short-lived glory associated with physical strength. However, man may not always have the option of exercising his power through mental activity; before age prompts him to rely on his brain as best he can, he can always count on his muscles and turn his body into a weapon.

Man does not hesitate to use force to establish his share of power. When he is not beating up his wife or his children, he gets into fights at the local; if he cannot be a soldier, he can always be a sportsman to show the world that he is a man, a real man. A smashed nose, missing teeth, prominent scars, a face swollen by blows or puffy from drugs: these are the real trophies of sporting competition. Sport is a territory where man feels at home, it is not a matter of playing but of fighting, of stretching himself to the limit. He takes pleasure in making his body into a good tool for battle and prepares himself through sport for the supreme virile activity: war. The rapier is no longer blunted, scrums are no longer bare-fisted: he can give free rein to exercising his power, and enjoying a real flirtation with death. In fire, fear and blood, the soldier at war experiences the strong sensations that only a 'real' man can rejoice in: 'I was a mortar and a machine gun specialist. I was very happy.' 'Later when I was recalled to go to Algeria, I was assigned to a battalion in the south-west where there were neither mortars nor machine guns. It was less fun.'[2]

So strong is his desire to be rid of his body that man sometimes succeeds in doing so, but he does not become the pure mind he likes to imagine: instead he ends up an invalid or a corpse. War and sport, of course, provide him ample opportunities to surpass himself – to fill the hospitals with the remains of his exploits, to enrich the earth with the bones of his glory. But he also finds scope in the most mundane activities: straddling his motorbike, for example, he enjoys risking a serious accident at every bend, or, downing five shorts in a row, he can show that he, a man, is not afraid of alcohol, even if his liver, his arteries and his stomach cannot take any more. What does it matter what the means and the end are, as long as the mutilated body shows signs of the heroic struggle man has waged against his fears and his own flesh?

Man does not always go to these extremes. In most cases he does not attach much importance to his appearance, and is happy to consider his body as a mere tool: the instrument of his mind. He usually sees this as the best way of guaranteeing his power; especially since in relying on his physical strength and appearance as little as possible, he manages to ensure that time is on his side. Not needing to be either strong or handsome, he is even less afraid of the ravages of old age; when his body deteriorates and his face creases with wrinkles, they are wrinkles of wisdom. And so old age becomes his final victory, not only over nature, but also over woman. Her faded beauty will evoke death and inspire disgust; his own features will radiate wisdom and experience.

Manly aesthetics

The way man treats his physical appearance and imposes feminine aesthetics on women is a good illustration of his attitude towards the body. It can be seen from clothes and from fashion in general, where virility and femininity express their different functions, heightening anatomical differences, increasing women's dependence and stressing anything that seems to represent human strength in the man.

Man identifies woman with nature and treats her accordingly: he tames and cultivates her. Just as he turns forests into fields and gardens, so he makes women into housewives and models. As woman is supposed to hold the key to all the dark and disturbing mysteries of the body, man seeks to give her a reassuring and seductive image. She represents the fear and disgust he feels for the flesh; by moulding her according to his own interests, he is trying to give her a reassuring form. And so when a woman takes off her pinafore she must be 'beautiful'; it is out of the question for her to be natural – she is supposed to be natural enough as it is. She must wear make up, be deodorised, perfumed, shave her legs and armpits, put on stockings, high-heels, show her legs, emphasise her breasts, pull in her stomach, paint her nails, dye her hair, tame her hairstyle, pierce her ears, reduce her appetite and, without making a single clumsy gesture, or uttering one word too many, she must seem happy, dainty and original.

By imposing femininity on women, man not only establishes his power and creates objects which are pleasant to behold, he also aims to produce, out of the restrictions and discomfort that women suffer, the inverted image of his own freedom and independence (the example used is one of fashion and dress, but we could also speak of mutilation, various forms of physical, intellectual and sexual violence, limiting or forbidding contraception and abortion, etc.): the more man restricts the freedom and well-being of a women through her body, the more he feels he is in control of his own body and certain of his pleasures. He is not dependent, as she is, on the fickleness of looks, on the flimsiness of a girdle or the precariousness of a stiletto heel; flabby, paunchy, bald or spotty, what does it matter? What is important for a man is what is in his head and his strength: he is not fallow flesh to be enhanced, but a mind, lord and master of his body. Make no mistake about it: the stronger sex is certainly not the fair sex!

One of the main purposes of clothing is to differentiate the sexes. The wearing of trousers is obligatory for western men and French law even forbids a man to wear a skirt or a dress outside carnival time; on the other hand, it is only recently that women have started wearing trousers. In France it was generally forbidden in high schools before 1968, and, even today, a woman who has to take an examination, or go to a job interview is advised not to wear trousers. She must show her legs and make her vagina accessible; whereas a man does not have to reveal his calves or offer easy access to his penis. One does not trifle with the accessories of the difference between the sexes; that is why, a few years ago, the Thai army radio, accusing the police of being 'soft' in the upholding of law and order, gave the following advice: 'the police chiefs ought to get a new uniform and swap their trousers for skirts.'[3]

The attitudes of the two sexes towards clothes are also completely different. Woman, supposed to exist only as a body, is expected to 'embellish' it, and 'personalise' it, to dress with a certain originality – to the extent that the same dress worn by two different women can transform a party into a disaster. Man, on the other hand, need not worry so much about his appearance, as it is of secondary importance to his mind or muscles; if he does pay any attention to his clothes it is to ensure that they symbolise his strength or conceal his flesh.

Mostly man seeks to let his body blend in to uniformity and to use dress as the symbol of his power. This ambitious project is usually realised in the army, which is the last stage in the initiation into the joys of virility. The minute he reports to army camp, man is greeted with the barber's clippers and a uniform:

not a hair must be out of place, no colour must clash; and, when they are all at attention, it must look like there is only one head. The purpose of military uniform is not only to standardise, it also symbolises strength and the exercise of power. The material and the colours, the boots and the clothes themselves – fatigues, battle-dress, parka, etc. – everything is designed for efficiency in battle. Of course, in civilian life, man is not this military caricature; even so, the colours he prefers are neutral and dull – grey, beige, dark brown, navy blue – and there is not much variety in style: he traditionally sports suit and tie, or for everyday wear, different variations of the eternal shapeless jacket, baggy trousers and heavy, uncomfortable shoes.

Still, it seems recently that a new outfit – jeans, bomber jackets and running shoes – has become increasingly popular. The colours are usually less sad but they remain pure – red, black, green, blue – and the clothing is tighter fitting. Apart from the ease and mobility it offers, this dress has the advantage of looking sporty, evoking strength and physical prowess. That is no doubt one of the main reasons for its success. Rather than comfort, he looks for an expression of his power in his clothes and accessories. Once again, the army is the best example of the masculine approach: the only touches which individualise the uniform are the stripes and decorations; these are so highly esteemed that leaders like Brezhnev, Bokassa or Amin Dada used to cover their chests with medals. And when man does not have, or no longer has, the opportunity of sticking decorations all over himself, he can still fall back on wearing a black leather jacket, or a president-style suit: anything will do to symbolise power.

Masculine elegance provides a good example of the way man asserts himself through standardisation and through control over his body. A distinguished or smart outfit is neither complicated nor very varied: it consists of a two- or three-piece suit in a (very) dark colour, black or dark-coloured shoes, a pale shirt, white, more often than not, dull socks and underwear. To round off the whole effect, a long thin band of material called a 'tie' is knotted under the chin. If the rest is not particularly comfortable the tie is downright unpleasant. To understand its presence, it must be remembered that the neck is a crucial point; the link between the head and the rest of the body – in short, in masculine imagery, it is the dividing line between the flesh and the mind. Therefore it is of utmost importance to draw attention to the boundary, and to try and eliminate the risk of a link being made, a garrotte is placed between the two. Thus, the tie is reassuring; just observe a man straightening his tie after a tricky situation– whew! that's better – he seems able to breathe again: his neck is tightly gripped, he is no more than a head suspended in the air.

As Charles Reich points out in *The Greening of America*: 'Sitting across from a man in a business suit, it is as if he did not have a body at all, just a face and a voice.' That is precisely the effect sought by the well-groomed man: but the face must not reveal a hint of sensuality, it must be nothing more than a receptacle for the brain. His face must not express a trace of innocence or neglect, and so he is clean-shaven and his hair is closely cropped; a humiliation which is sometimes inflicted on women, but for the man it is the confirmation of his power. As one general said, at a time when there was a slight wave of protest in the French army: 'You will not ride twice in a tank with long hair!'

It seems that over the last few years, a new attitude towards masculine aesthetics has developed. Some of the people in charge are worried – will it be possible to tell men from women, is man becoming effeminate? So far it is not too serious; in the sixties, young people simply refused to camouflage their corporality under a white shirt or submit to the barber's razor: a rejection of the clean-cut close shave. Masculine hair was worn much longer, clothes became less drab and more comfortable, and, to the rhythm of rock music, masculine aesthetics took a step forward.

From the Beatles, who caused a scandal for setting the trend for 'long' hair, to David Bowie and Lou Reed who went in for transvestism, including Mick Jagger and the Californian rock groups at the end of the sixties, man's image has undergone some changes. But in spite of appearances (and not forgetting the backlash that has taken place since – macho fashion: tie, close-cropped hair, black leather, pointed boots etc.) virility has remained intact. To the classic insult 'With your long hair you look like a woman', the answer was, for example, very rarely 'That's true. It's good – why don't you try it?' but rather 'That doesn't mean anything, I'm still a man, I am, mate.' And, if the balance of power and the tension were sufficient, this altercation could easily end in a fight. Moreover, to avoid any ambiguity or error, long hair was quickly accompanied by irrefutable proof or virility: sideburns, beard or moustache – clear emblems – and often heavy boots, leather jacket and a mean expression were added for good measure.

Similarly, the beauty industry, sensing the change, began a long-term offensive aimed at men. Since their favourite field, woman's body, was almost totally colonised – from the most 'intimate' parts to the most 'feminine' days – they could only maintain their expansion rate by using imagination and extending their market to include products for men. From the beginning, it was a matter of not being too ambitious, and gradually easing men on from shaving products towards deodorants and perfumes. The principal line of attack was first of all to rid perfume of its exclusively feminine character so that it could become a new attribute of virility. Not a simple task, and the advertisers used kid gloves to put over the message – 'Don't worry, if you wear perfume, you won't become sensual and desirable but sporty and elegant, virile and refined. You will smell clean and tough, you won't become a woman; on the contrary, you'll be even more of a man.' Everything has been used, from the most virile-sounding names – Brut, Victor, Mandate – to the most varied male images – from Don Juan to Henry Cooper. With slogans like 'the great smell of Brut', the path has been cleared, man has picked up the scent.

Over the last few years stylishness has become a new facet of virility, which now tends to adopt the more flexibe name of 'masculinity'. Perfume and elegance, once the prerogative of the aristocrat and the bourgeois, have been democratised on the body of the trendy young executive. The man who knows how 'to live' nowadays is increasingly elegant, he has exchanged his plain white pants and vest for red, yellow or striped ones, his suits have got a little lighter and are cut to follow the contours of his body, his hair is longer and more attention is paid to the style. What is more, he invariably leaves in his wake a fresh and discreet smell, the product of various syntheses of modern chemistry.

The market has kept pace. Boutiques for 'him' are opening and prospering everywhere; small local barbers with their clippers are being replaced, little by little, by much more sophisticated hairdressing salons; and on street corners, advertisements of half-naked men showing off the colours of their new underpants can be seen. But here the advertisers become very cautious again, they know that they must not go too far; in France in 1967 an advertisement showing the blurred silhouette of a naked man in semi-darkness caused an outcry, and since then too much masculine nudity has been avoided. It is a matter of not confusing the genders: the body which is plastered-naked over walls, photographed from every angle and in every position, is that of the woman – on the rare posters where man exposes his flesh, not only is he wearing underpants but he keeps his running shoes on or wears a grimace of physical exertion; and if by chance he risks a slightly suggestive pose, then it is balanced by *The Times* in his hand.

The beauty industry is cautious in its approach; for them, it is not a matter of questioning the sex categories but of exploiting them to the utmost and using any means available to play on the frustrations these categories bring about. Thus, the mechanisms for exploiting women through femininity have been highly polished and the dividends pay off regularly; as for man, the offensive is barely under way when already a new masculinity is rising over the horizon and it seems clear that to sell him 'a right to beauty', when he is bogged down in the uniformity of his dress and hatred for his body, will prove to be an excellent prospect to exploit.

Desiring to be a woman

Man sometimes finds it difficult to fit the mould. His own mutilation leaves him with a somewhat confused sensation of loss:

he longs to feel his body alive, fragile and beautiful. The frustration of seeing his body as only ugly and lifeless generally prompts him to be fascinated by woman's body, or rather by a certain image which he makes into a symbol of beauty, life and fragility. This fascination is one of the forces behind his heterosexual desire – to appropriate beauty through the appropriation, the 'possession' of a woman – but it can also be expressed in a desire to wear women's clothes or to acquire the anatomical characteristics of the female sex.

Dressing as the opposite sex is the logical consequence of being confined within sex categories: it is one of the ways of trying to get out of it, and is, no doubt, as old as the categories themselves. The Old Testament, for example, refers to it: 'No woman shall wear an article of man's clothing, nor shall a man put on woman's dress; for those who do these things are abominable to the Lord your God.' (*Deuteronomy* XXII:5)

In spite of the taboos and legal prohibitions, it is rare for man not to give in, at least once in his life, to the temptation to look like a woman. A fancy-dress ball, a party, or the simple intimacy of a mirror all afford the opportunity of putting on the characteristics of femininity – bra, skirt, tights – of wearing make-up, or making his penis disappear between crossed thighs. Dressing as a woman is a favourite form of entertainment among men: thus, during a party at the military academy of Saint-Cyr, De Gaulle, who was at the time a trainee officer, got married to one of his comrades – however, probably because of his height, the future general did not play the part of the bride – and more recently, sailors from the liner *France*, taking advantage of the occupation of their ship, threw themselves into dressing up as 'Moulin Rouge cabaret girls'. 'A bad impression', commented the journalist from *Le Monde*.[4] Nevertheless, it is true that when he dares take the plunge, man likes to wear woman's clothing and sometimes he wants to dress as a woman for longer than just one evening.

It is not very difficult to borrow the accessories of femininity: clothes, shoes or wigs, make-up, hair removers, and even padded bras, hormones, silicone, electrolysis or plastic surgery; man only has to use the same means as woman to become a 'real woman' (including the most sophisticated techniques, like the different surgical operations to create perfect breasts, which are very often used by women whose bodies must symbolise feminine beauty: dancers, strip-tease artistes, actresses and models). In fact the problem of the transvestite who does not want to be recognised as such, is not how to transform himself into a woman, but how to avoid overdoing it.

For several years, the man who has decided to make his body resemble woman's as closely as possible has also been able to resort to surgery to transform his penis and testicles into a sort of vulva extended into a vagina. These operations are quite common in the United States, Morocco and in England, and individuals who have modified the criteria which assign them to a sex category, are sometimes allowed to change their legal status. There are many famous cases in Anglo-Saxon countries. In 1978, for the first time in France, three changes in civil status were granted by provincial tribunals. Somehow or other, when man manages to be recognised in his daily life as a woman, he can then hold jobs such as cashier, factory girl, hairdresser or typist, and even become a wife. But if he is refused legal recognition and he is short of money, the feminine image which most often attracts the transsexual and the transvestite is that of the woman as an object of contemplation which kindles desire in the man; and she is generally on a stage or walking the streets.

Transvestite shows have always been highly successful. Man, who rarely dares live out his desire to dress up in woman's clothes, is fond of going to watch those who do it professionally on the stage; however, not feeling necessarily at ease faced with a body which he knows to be masculine, he generally prefers to laugh rather than desire. The entertainment world knows this, and most transvestite numbers are comic – ridiculous get-ups, exaggerated poses, parody – so that in fact the transvestite is not regarded as a woman, but as a transvestite; and man laughs more often than he gets a hard-on. Prostitution, on the other hand, offers real opportunities: by specialising in oral sex, the transvestite can be approached and treated 'like a woman'. Obviously, even if he has already had a breast operation, the situation carries the risk that a wandering hand might not be content just to fondle his breasts – which are so 'perfect' – and want to descend towards his genitals; then the reaction is unpredictable, and not necessarily violent. The encounter may end up with one of those good old conversations between men.

Indeed, whatever he does to become a 'woman', and even if he occasionally manages to carry it off, the transvestite nevertheless remains socially a 'man'. Even the transsexual will never really be considered as a woman but always as a man trying to pass himself off as a woman. Neither of them can escape the 'man' category, they are merely the exceptions who confirm the rules.

Through transvestism and transsexuality, man tries in vain to throw off virility; he will risk anything – simple jeering, brutal social rejection, serious physical mutilation – to no longer be a 'man'. He deeply feels the frustration of being locked in a definition. But he does not usually find himself as a transvestite, as it is not in to himself, physically male, that he looks; all he does is try and imitate. Dazzled by 'woman', fascinated by femininity, he yearns to have those breasts, that vulva and that womb which he sees as symbols of the life, the beauty and the sensuality that he does not see in himself.

When man feels ill at ease in his masculine body, which he does not always want to sacrifice on the altar of virile glory, it rarely occurs to him that he can discover life and beauty, fragility and sensuality in his own body. He generally prefers to try, as if by magic, to make it sensual by copying a female stereotype.

Man struggles within his body, he seeks to free himself from it, but he generally gets his priorities wrong. It is not through fragmenting it or mutilating it that he will become independent and feel good in himself, but by accepting it as it is. Whether he wants it or not, his body is no more that tool which he tries to make into an instrument of power than the flesh which he tries to render attractive beneath a feminine appearance: it is simply an integral part of himself.

It is not through the symbols of femininity that man will regain his integrity, his lost 'rib'. On the contrary, his freedom and the diversity of his pleasures begin beyond the sexual dichotomy: an unshaven face no longer has anything masculine about it, it can simply be the desire not to irritate the cheeks with a razor blade too often; a skirt no longer has anything feminine about it because it is pleasant to feel your legs free under the material, or because you enjoy, on a summer evening, to feel the warm air between the thighs. Anything is possible outside the definitions 'masculine' and 'feminine', and it is highly likely that the obsessive desire for the female body, be it to appropriate it or to imitate it, would no longer weigh on the male who could glimpse the potential of his own body when released from confinement in a sex category.

3. Man and his penis

The sexual organ is not only the anatomical feature which most obviously differentiates males and females, it is also the criterion which divides human being into men and women. And so it is hardly surprising that man attaches great importance to the testicles and bit of flesh dangling between his legs, because they actually bestow power on him. He has therefore made them the symbols of his power, and erected landmarks everywhere in the image of his victories; he has covered the earth with phalluses which increase in height as construction technology improves. The Egyptian obelisks are doubtless the most sophisticated, that is, that bear the least likeness; and nowadays there is really no shortage of phalluses pointing up towards the sky – in Paris alone, there is one for everybody: the Bastille is for the people, The Vendôme column is for the bourgeois, the technocrats have the Montparnasse Tower, and so that no one feels left out, the tourists have the Eiffel Tower.

On this basis, man has directly reproduced his imagery of man as culture and woman as nature on the sexual organs: he has located the penis on a human scale, and the woman as a force of nature against which he fights through her vagina. Following the traditional metaphor of the phallus as a plough-share furrowing the woman, he has diversified the imagery: with the knife blade, the barrel of a gun, or the electric drill, the vagina has become either the wound he opens or the hole he bores. His morbid imagination has produced a batch of endless metaphors, which, however, come up against the anatomical and physiological reality of the two sex organs: the vagina is no more a hole or a wound than the penis is a tool or a weapon.

Ignorance and mutilation

For a long time woman's sex organ was considered by scientists to be 'nothing' in itself; the vulva being only the entrance to the vagina, which in turn was a mere recipient for the penis. It was only in the twentieth century that in the West it was recognised in scientific circles that not only did woman have a sex organ but also that it functioned, anatomically, more or less like a man's. Kinsey remarks, in *Sexual Behaviour in the Human Female*:

> In brief, we conclude that the anatomic structures which are most essential to sexual response and orgasm, are nearly identical in the human female and male. The differences are relatively few. They are associated with the different functions of the sexes in reproductive processes, but they are of no great significance in the origins and development of sexual response and orgasm.[1]

More recently, the sexologists Masters and Johnson have also emphasised the similarity between the physiological reactions in the male and the female genital organs.

> The parallels in reaction to effective sexual stimulation emphasise the physiologic similarities in male and female responses rather than the differences. Aside from obvious anatomic variants, men and women are homogenous in their physiologic responses to sexual stimuli.[2]

Taking clinical observations and recent research as a basis, it is possible to compare the reactions of the two sexual organs during sexual stimulation. It is obviously not a matter of going into a detailed description of all the anatomical reactions of the various elements which compose the genital organs – labia, clitoris, scrotum, testicles, etc. – we shall concentrate only on the movements of the vagina and the penis, as they are the two organs which the male imagination focuses on.

As far as the vagina is concerned, any sexual stimulation causes a rush of blood and induces a discharge; the vagina secretes and grows noticeably in size. As the excitement becomes more intense, a fresh rush of blood causes the external third to dilate, this is what Masters and Johnson call the 'orgasmic plateau'; in other words, it becomes firmer and takes on a more definite shape. Finally, during orgasm, it contracts frequently and regularly around the orgasmic plateau, and then little by little it goes back to its usual shape. As for the penis, it follows more or less the same pattern; except that behavioural manifestations are external and there is no mucoid secretion. In response to stimulation the blood vessels dilate and the penis becomes enlarged; then a second rush of blood slightly increases the circumference, mainly around the coronal ridge and during orgasm, like the vagina, it contracts at regular intervals – incidentally, the rhythm of the contractions is the same – then it gradually goes back to its regular shape.

And so, anatomically and physiologically, the two organs are very similar; and yet this has not stopped man from ignoring the vagina and regarding it as a mere inert hole, or from being almost entirely ignorant concerning his own penis, which he sees as a power symbol and an instrument of sexual appropriation. Quite obviously man does not know his own genitals, and now science has recognised this. Masters and Johnson, no doubt wishing to make up for lost time, comment:

> The functioning role of the penis is as well established as that of any other organ in the body. Ironically, there is no organ about which more misinformation has been perpetrated. The penis constantly has been viewed but rarely seen. The organ has been venerated, reviled and misrepresented with intent in art, literature and legend through the centuries . . . These 'phallic fallacies' have colored our arts, and possibly, of even more import to our culture, influenced our behavioural and biologic sciences . . . Why . . . should the functional role of the penis have been shrouded so successfully by the 'phallic fallacy' concepts? This, indeed, is one of the great mysteries of biologic science.[3]

Is it really so mysterious? How indeed can these 'phallic fallacies' be avoided, when the penis is precisely the organ that determines membership of the man class. Man turns a little bit

of soft, delicate and highly sensitive flesh into the factor which
bestows power on him; he is blind to the warmth, the fragility
and the hypersensitivity of his penis, he represents it as cold,
hard and sharp as a blade. It becomes a symbol and instrument
of power. He forces himself to control it and tries to separate it
from the rest of his body; often even mutilating himself in practising a symbolic separation through circumcision.

Circumcision is a mutilation practised widely through the
world, and doubtless has different purposes in the different
societies where it is a ritual. Bruno Bettelheim, based on his
studies of schizophrenic children and pre-literate peoples,[4]
believes it could be, for example, 'a male substitute for girls'
first menstrual cycle'. This hypothesis may be true in some cases
but it does not shed any light on the real purpose of mutilation
in the history of Judeo-Christian patriarchy.

Yet the institution of circumcision plays an important part in
the Old Testament. A few chapters after the description of the
mythical separation of man from his phallus-snake, it seems in
fact, like the symbolic separation that man engraves in his own
flesh, his 'covenant' with God:

> God said to Abraham, 'For your part you must keep my
> covenant, you and your descendants after you; circumcise
> yourselves, every male among you. You shall circumcise
> the flesh of your foreskin, and it shall be the sign of the
> covenant between us.' (*Genesis* XVII: 9–11)

The other condition of the 'covenant', the advantages gained
– i.e. the point of the mutilation – is presented quite straight-
forwardly:

> As an everlasting possession I will give you and your
> descendants after you the land in which you now are
> aliens, all the land of Canaan, and I will be God to your
> descendants. (*Genesis* XVII: 8)

Thus circumcision is established as the price man must pay
not only in order to assert his power as father, leader and pro-

prietor, but also to perpetuate and extend it, from one generation to the next, by handing it down from father to son. It is in fact the rite through which man generates supremacy; and he forces it on his son almost immediately after his birth: 'Every male among you in every generation shall be circumcised on the eighth day.' (*Genesis* XVII: 12) The Old Testament has revived a marriage initiation rite, practised among the ancient Hebrews at the time of betrothal, and by applying it to new-born males, made it the sign of the covenant with God. The mutilation of the penis was no longer the last stage of initiation into 'manhood' before taking a wife, it became the very symbol of man's power, inscribed on his penis from the earliest age.

Thus, in the history of Judeo-Christian ideology, circumcision is the baton through which the father passes his power on to his son. I can't agree with Bettelheim's theory that one of the purposes of the rite is 'to pretend that men too can bear children',[5] as it is not the ability to reproduce life that man is concerned with when mutilating his son's penis, but rather the reproduction of power. Nor is circumcision, as Freud supposed, 'the symbolical substitute of castration, a punishment which the primeval father dealt his sons long ago with the fullness of his power.'[6] On the contrary, it is the transmission of the father's power to the son.

The separation from his penis, which man achieves mythically in the description of original sin, and symbolically through circumcision, has nothing to do with castration. Its purpose is diametrically opposed. Castration is the removal of the symbol of power and the instrument of sexual appropriation – it was, for example, in certain cultures, inflicted on the defeated enemy by the victors who secured a trophy celebrating their triumph and, at the same time, removed the criterion of the power from men who, now they were slaves, were no longer entitled to it. Circumcision, on the other hand, is an attempt to make the symbol more convincing and the instrument more effective. By mutilating his son's penis, the father engraves the symbolic image of the sacrifice of sexuality in the struggle for power, in his son's flesh.

Christianity later abolished this rite to replace it with the image, considered more eloquent, of the sacrifice of the entire body. Since the Son became the Father under the strokes of the hammer nailing his limbs to the cross, man no longer had to pay for his future right to his father's power with the strokes of the flint cutting through his foreskin. The symbolic mutilation as a preparation to the assumption of power was replaced by the mythical sacrifice, which justifies all the real sacrifices in the power race.

Yet, using medical pretexts, Christians today are tending to return to the practice of circumcision. The removal of the foreskin obviously loses its symbolic significance; but, under the surgeon's scalpel whose object is to make the penis 'cleaner' and 'more suitable' for its purpose, it is still an attempt to improve the instrument through mutilation.

The symbol of power

Man's misfortune is that his penis, the symbol of power, is, in fact, one of the most fragile and vulnerable organs of his body. In spite of all his efforts to strengthen it, his penis remains his weak spot: the target to aim for to annihilate his strength. Man has such difficulty recovering from a blow in the groin that he has to protect it when practising violent sports, and, in fights, punches below the belt are forbidden – a prohibition which can become brutal when a woman intervenes:

> When two men are fighting, and the wife of one of them comes near to drag her husband clear of his opponent, if she puts out her hand and catches hold of the man's genitals, you shall cut off her hand and show her no mercy. (*Deuteronomy* XXV: 11–12)

Man is embarrassed by the vulnerability of his penis. He often finds it ridiculous in its normal state – the penis and testicles with their gentle swaying are more reminiscent of the udders of a half-starved goat than the instrument of power that he wants to have between his legs. Man neither accepts nor truly appreciates his penis unless it is in state of erection. It then seems to him less fragile, and its movements more controllable: it seems to harden like an ordinary biceps. And in this state it is ready to act as an instrument of appropriation: it becomes the necessary weapon with which to approach a woman.

Man is often ill at ease when faced with his own nudity. When he undresses in front of a woman, he often keeps on his underpants, only removing them when protected by the intimacy of the sheets – or as soon as he has an erection. For the situation is then different; he is brandishing the image of his power, and can enter the battlefield of love preceded by his standard bearer.

The erect penis is the weapon man arms himself with to try and tame a woman via her vagina; and so he tries to make it threatening, and he likes it to arouse fear. This attitude is illustrated by the behaviour of the flasher. He walks the streets to expose, unexpectedly, his erect member, to women on their own: his pleasure is in the astonishment and fear which he provokes, and in their haste to flee his assault; if on the other hand, the woman merely walks past him giving him a contemptuous look or offering to go up and see his etchings, then it is he who is overcome with fear, he loses his proud hard-on and takes flight all tangled up in his flies. Of course man rarely practises exhibitionism systematically. Nevertheless, he does enjoy the feeling that his penis can frighten women: he sees the image of his own power reflected in the woman's fear as she trembles before the threatening weapon.

The use to which man puts his penis, and the instruments with which he identifies it, suggest size as a measure of efficacity; to such an extent that it is his main worry where his penis is concerned. He sees it as a sort of biceps, the bigger it is, the stronger it must be – therefore the more powerful he is. But if the proportions of muscles can be increased by training, and are generally perceptible to the naked eye, it is not so in the case of the penis; and the question of whether or not his penis compares favourably with others often poses a problem which man has difficulty in settling. And so it is not rare for him to ask a woman, with a note of apprehension, to compare his penis with her former lovers' – is his better than average or not? The question haunts and worries him so much that sometimes he consults an expert to reassure himself. Those of *Union, The International Review of Human Relations*, a magazine edited by doctors of medicine, psychology and philosophy, were only too pleased to oblige:

> **Q** – And also, I have always been overcome with a sort of anxiety . . . when flaccid the dimensions of my penis vary according to the situation, sometimes hanging, sometimes contracted, on average 7cm long and 11cm in circumference. On the other hand, when erect it is 15cm long and 13cm in circumference. I am 1 metre 80 tall, and I have always felt that, in comparison with others, my penis was rather small. Are you planning to deal with this subject in the near future?
> **A** – We have decided to invent a new taboo: that of the centimetre. We forbid all our readers to measure penises. Masters and Johnson have shown, after scientific research, that the size of the penis has nothing to do with sexual capacity.

It was not long, however, before they returned to the question. About two months later the cover of the seventh issue announced: 'The Scientific Study of the Penis'. One could reasonably have expected, after what had been said, a detailed study of the sensitivity, warmth and pleasures of the male genitalia . . . but this attitude was short-lived. The title of *Union*'s article eloquently shows where they're at. 'Study of the penis: The results of an enquiry concerning the measurements of the penis according to age, race and marital status, height and weight.'

The editorial staff of *Union* no doubt wished to relax the rigorous 'new taboo' inflicted on its readership; it even offered them a much more precise way to measure themselves than the modest centimetre:

> For each group of measurements we have calculated what we call the CVI: the comparative volume of the penis

index. Expressed in cubic centimetres, this figure, which should be considered more as an indication than the exact evaluation of the real volume of the penis, was obtained by considering simply the shaft of the erect penis as a cylinder whose circumference could be calculated by taking the average of two specified measurements, and the glans as a hemisphere with the same circumference at the base. By multiplying the length by the circumference we obtained the approximate volume of the organ. To obtain a more precise estimate it would have been necessary to take into account the diverse variations in form of the erect penis, but that would have involved much more numerous and complete measurements.[7]

However, man does not always have a specialist review at hand, and even then, comparisons are delicate; anyway, whom does one compare oneself to, and what is the norm? The first reference is of course to the father whose penis is directly associated with power, but the dimensions of which are a jealously guarded secret in most cases. Attempting to find out can even lead to severe retaliation. One of Noah's sons, Ham, was cursed through his descendants for ever because he took advantage of his father's drunken sleep to satisfy his curiosity about the patriarch's 'nakedness'.

Man usually becomes very shy about his penis; as he is rarely sure of the quality of its size, he prefers to hide it rather than risk exposing himself to ridicule because his penis might be 'smaller than average'. This shyness makes it even more difficult to find out what the norm is. Not only is it hard for man to get information but, what is more, when an opportunity arises he is torn between his desire to find out and his fear of exposing himself. In the changing rooms of a sportsground or a swimming pool, for example, his modesty usually gets the better of him – especially if he is undressing in front of strangers. However, the most ridiculous situation is usually in public lavatories: man often feels trapped in front of the urinal, between his urge to see, his fear of being seen and the worry that over-curiosity will put in doubt his heterosexuality; so obsessed is he with the little bit of flesh which surrounds his uretha, that he relieves himself, but he does not relax. Man makes an organ which could be so practical for urinating into a symbol of power, and sometimes he pees over his fingers in his attempts to hide its size from prying eyes.

The tribulations associated with dimensions are the routine of virility. For many men, success equals a big penis– 'The size of my penis determines my behaviour and my behaviour determines the size of my penis.' It is hardly an exaggeration to say that relations between men are reduced to a competition in penis size. Whether in politics, war, sport or relationships with women, man is always competing; he is fond of relations involving a duel, and the slightest excuse to measure himself will do. Of course, once he has outgrown adolescence, he rarely uses a ruler; the sword and the revolver of old can be replaced by the knife and the razor blade. But the duel today generally takes on a more subtle form, for instance, in conversation, and it has found an excellent battleground in consumption. But in spite of the various transformations the duel has undergone through the ages, one of the favourite instruments of measurement has nevertheless remained woman. The principle is simple: as the penis is supposed to be a sort of biceps, the more it is used, the larger it will become; in the same way the bigger it is, the better it can subdue women, thus the more successful the man is likely to be. We have come full circle – a big penis guarantees success and success guarantees a big penis.

When man forgets his measurements and gives free rein to his fantasies, the size of his penis generally acquires frenzied proportions. Erotic literature for example, offers a profusion of big pricks, enormous members, formidable cocks, superb tools proudly erect, huge truncheons, powerful dicks, magnificent swords, splendid rods.

In reality, one of man's greatest misfortunes with his penis, apart from the fact that he cannot maintain it in a state of erection, is that he cannot enlarge it like other muscles. And so, as he has not yet found an effective way of making it bigger – the devices invented so far are more useful for masturbating than as expanders – he sometimes devotes himself to experiments to improve his performance. Sometimes he goes to great lengths. Doctor Reuben cites 'ampallang' practised in South East Asia:[8]

> The sportier males of that area make several slits in the loose skin on the underside of the penis near the tip. The openings average about an eighth of an inch in diameter and run at right angles to the shaft. Just before intercourse, short rods are inserted into the slits perpendicular to the penis. These are usually scraps of copper wire, bits of ivory, or among the jet set, gold and silver . . . For those willing to go one step further, there is a somewhat more elegant refinement. Instead of simply poking holes in the organ, a ring of small incisions is made around the head of the penis. Little pebbles are placed into the resulting pouches, and the skin is allowed to heal over them. A month or so later, the result is a penis crowned with a rocky wreath. Fully healed, the courageous gent emerges to claim his reward; presumably the girls are standing in line to get the benefit of this new equipment. A plain old normal penis must look pretty tame by comparison.

Nowadays, thanks to the enormous progress of Western civilisation, the catalogues of erotic accessories offer condoms making it possible to avoid these painful mutilations. These come in shapes which are sufficiently varied to satisfy the most unusual tastes: these include not only the inevitable double-overhead camshaft, but also a spiral staircase winding round a gasometer, or a figurine resembling Napoleon at the top of a column cast in gun-metal.

Man does not like his penis: he is not very interested in its delights and pleasures; he wishes to dissociated himself from it; and whether he hides it or whether he brandishes it, leaves it as it is or improves it, he neglects its potential. He does not see the softness of the glans, the fragility and extreme excitability of the frenum, the sensitivity of the shaft along the urethra, the rough tenderness of the scrotum. He tries, on the contrary, to desensitise the whole organ as best he can to give it the coldness and the hardness of metal. What he loses in enjoyment he hopes to compensate for in power; but if he gains an undeniable power symbol, what pleasure can he really feel with a *weapon* between his legs?

4. Man and sexuality

Man does not allow his sexuality to develop fully, he stifles it by confining it to his penis. He projects it onto woman by making her into a sexual creature. The role attributed to Eve in the Bible illustrates this as does the Ancient Greek myth of Pandora who is held responsible for all the evils on earth after opening her 'box'. But one of the best illustrations of his attitude is the way man compares male and female pleasure and marvels at the potential for orgasm with which he credits woman.

One of the earliest experts at comparison was probably Tiresias, the Greek soothsayer who is said to have turned himself into a woman in order to formulate an unbiased judgement. His conclusion was categorical: woman's orgasm is nine times as intense as a man's. Subsequently, such perfect sex changes have become rarer, but that has not prevented men's imaginations from making comparisons. Montaigne,[1] for example, has no qualms in assuring men that women 'are incomparably more capable and more ardent than we in the act of love'. A few centuries later 'M'[2] also warns us: 'I am most distressed to have to tell you this, but sexually speaking, we are mistaken if we think we are the stronger sex. Women are capable of having orgasms ten times as intense as ours.' Even more recently, Pascal Bruckner and Alain Finkielkraut in *Le Nouveau Désordre Amoureux*, observe that in comparison with 'the sad simplicity of male pleasure', woman's orgasm is like: 'a small-scale production of the creation of the universe'.

All these comparisons set the tone: man does not see the richness of his own sexuality and decrees that sex is woman. Obviously this does not imply that a woman may enjoy her supposed extraordinary sexuality in her own way, but, on the contrary, the pleasure that a man keeps for himself is precisely that of power, in particular, power over woman's pleasure. Man feels sexual pleasure as a threat to his power; he controls and channels it as best he can for fear of being submerged by pleasure. He is at sixes and sevens: he sees its domination as a way of dominating nature; but whereas sexuality is essentially letting-go, communication and delight, he represents it as self-control, struggle and a means of asserting his power.

The music of power

His general attitude is shown in the language he uses: he fucks and she gets fucked; he portrays heterosexual relationships based on this theme through images which are as graphic as they are varied. The most common is of course that of the violinist, the violin and bow – the traditional trio – the man, the woman and the phallus. The relationship is clear: the violin produces harmonious notes which melt into the air, but without the violinist and his bow, it is nothing more than a beautiful, curvaceous object, a mere promise of music. It quivers but cannot choose the rhythm or the melody; it is dependent, body and soul, on the musician, on his skill, his mood and his sensitivity. The comparison is striking and it has been used unsparingly. Simone de Beauvoir quotes both Balzac, 'Woman is like a lyre which gives up its secret only to him who knows how to play on it,' and Jules Guyot, 'He is the player who produces either harmony or cacophony with his hand and his bow. Woman is, from this point of view, verily a stringed instrument that will produce either harmonious or discordant sounds according to how well it is tuned.'[3]

However, man does not always have a musical ear, in which case he can choose from a vast range of metaphors: he can identify with the hunter, weapon in hand, confronting his most dangerous quarry, woman; the toreador in the bull-ring, feeling reassured by the presence of his sword, knowing he will soon deliver the final thrust; the sweating gymnast performing tirelessly until he has worn out his vaulting horse; the warrior after the siege, breaking down the draw-bridge with his battering ram and forcing his way as victor into the conquered stronghold. There is no shortage of metaphors, and they all originate from man's obsession with dominating sexuality through woman and dominating woman through sexuality.

Man imagines his fulfilment not really in the pleasure he could experience, but rather in the obstacles he overcomes; sometimes he even goes as far as to create difficulties in order to assert himself. Knowing that the outcome is never certain goads him on in his struggle. Just as he may be wounded by the animal, engulfed by the sea, spurned by the mountain, so may he be refused or bewitched by woman. And so, although he is tempted by his dreams of conquest and adventure, man is often happy to sit back and admire the success of those who have realised them successfully. Of course, he is fascinated by the image of the violin and the violinist, but he generally prefers not to take risks, not everyone is a virtuoso. He purely and simply ignores woman's pleasure and reduces his own to mere ejaculation. Man can easily relieve his sexual needs thanks to three institutions deeply rooted in patriarchy: marriage, prostitution, and rape.

Marriage offers all the advantages and security of ownership. By getting married man appropriates, often for life, a woman who, in exchange for the means of subsistence, not only looks after his material and emotional needs, but also provides an on-the-spot sexual service which is guaranteed in the marital contract. This takes different forms in different patriarchal societies; in the West it has been institutionalised through Christianity as a duty which, if not performed, can lead to the marriage being annulled. The church has firmly instilled this through an ideological sleight of hand portraying woman as a sexual creature responsible for the evils of mankind. On these grounds her sexuality is repressed until it becomes an obligation, imposed from her wedding night onwards, subject to the desires of her husband. Thus, man is guaranteed, in the matrimonial bed, satisfaction whenever he wishes. Even so, man may occasionally feel inclined to indulge a few whims, or may be reluctant to make a long-term commitment by getting married – prostitution then enables him to satisfy his needs just as easily.

Prostitution offers all the advantages of being a tenant rather than a landlord: variety of choice, less bother and the opportunity to let yourself go a little at less expense. Besides, man enjoys the sensation of danger and power he experiences with a prostitute. With her he escapes from the daily routine, he is confronting 'sex' and he is playing with fire. He gets security from the fact that he is paying. He likes to feel that he retains the freedom to take the initiative through money, that he can desire without being rejected; sometimes he spends hours wandering around the red-light districts, looking, comparing, weighing up possibilities, delighting in seeing women on display waiting only for him. He feels in control of the situation: he believes he can choose any one he wants, when he wants, to do whatever he wants. Of course, from time to time he goes upstairs, comes, and feels better. But that means breaking the spell and he prefers often not to venture into the room, but to bask in the feeling of power he experiences walking among women for hire.

Sometimes, man feels sufficiently sure of himself with prostitutes to let himself go a little further than usual. He might even feel the urge to go a long way, but because he is first and foremost a 'man', and is therefore sexually inhibited, his way of experiencing intensity has nothing to do with pleasure; he expresses it through violence or pain. Many prostitutes have been injured, even murdered. On the other hand, there are occasions when violence is inflicted on men, but in this case it is controlled and chosen. A prostitute gives this description of male masochism:

> My masochist clients are rather special. They are usually men who are educated, who've got money and have some pretty unbelievable vices. They want us to beat them, or crush cigarettes out on their nipples, stick pins in their penises, drag them round the room by a string tied round the tip of their tongue, defecate over their mouths, insult them. And they reply: 'yes mistress', 'all right mistress' . . . I am often dressed in black, I never smile. I even wear black glasses, sometimes. I must wear high-

heels. It's very important. At home I have all the
paraphernalia: whips, chains, dildos, handcuffs . . .
Slaps, insults, strokes of the cat o'nine tails or the whip
cost a hundred quid. The whole show, sodomy, etc., costs
double. That's a hell of a lot of money. The longest it lasts
is half an hour, sometimes a little more, up to an hour. In
that case, the bloke leaves completely knackered,
it'll take him a month to get over his injuries. The punters
are really hurt, they have to heal afterwards. We can't
pretend to hurt them, it has to be real. Especially when
we stick pins into their penises, they bleed a lot because
when they come all the blood rises, and when you
take out the pins, it all gushes out. For this operation you
have to pull the skin taut with elastic bands so as not catch
any skin, stretch it well, and then stick the pins in. While
you're doing this they don't cry out, they moan, they're
getting a kick out of it. (Claude Jaget, *Une Vie de putain*,
Paris, Les Presses d'aujourd'hui, 1975)

Man tends to experience the intensity of his pleasure more
often through his own violence. When he gives in to his desires
he generally feels the urge to rape or be brutal. He satisfies
these wishes on a large scale during war. Not content with kill-
ing each other, soldiers are prepared to do anything for amuse-
ment including pillage and rape. Susan Brownmiller cites the
most atrocious example of brutality during the last few years:
Bangladesh, where, in 1971, Pakistani soldiers raped between
two and four hundred thousand women during their nine-
month campaign.[4]

However, man does not confine himself to the opportunities
provided by war. He sometimes expresses his pleasure in rape
and violence in his daily life. And even if he does not always
commit rape, it is nonetheless frequently on his mind: he fanta-
sises about it, and goes to see it portrayed at the cinema. It
represents something beyond the commodity relationship codified by marriage or prostitution: it is the appropriation of a
woman without having to give her anything in return. It
enables him to satisfy his desires without giving up his power.

It is the very expression of that power.

Rape and eroticism

Rape is the archetype of masculine sexuality; when man desires, woman is not to desire or refuse, she must only acquiesce. Whether in pyjamas, as the husband imposing conjugal rights, or in army fatigues forcing his way into an enemy village, man is not accustomed to giving woman any say in the matter: either with tears in his eyes or with a sub-machine gun in his hand, he knows how to get his own way. Rape is so common that man almost feels that it does not exist, like the barrister, a few years ago, who declared during the trial of three rapists: 'Is not the sexual freedom flaunted by the women an encouragement?' This was taken up in the letters page of the left-wing Paris daily, *Libération*: 'And what about the woman's responsibility in her own rape? . . . not wearing a bra, wearing tight-fitting jeans, perfume and make-up, are these not a provocation?'[5] The answer is contained in the way the question is phrased: if man rapes it is because woman asks for it, therefore it is not rape – this kind of logic is historically deeply rooted in the masculine mind, as this little dialogue from Euripides shows:

Helen: Thou diest, and I, woe's me, shall wed perforce.
Menelaus: Thou shouldst be traitress – false the plea of force.[6]

In fact man likes to think that violence is the pretext woman has been waiting for to let herself be appropriated; and so he can rape without any qualms and with a clear conscience. Man likes to invent the idea that woman has a rape fantasy which complements his own, and sometimes he even goes so far as to claim that he himself cannot wait to be raped. This mental juggling enables him to embellish reality and to disguise the fact that rape, more than being a mental game, is the very real appropriation of a human being through violence and under no circumstances can it be described as a pleasant experience for its victims.

Man should be aware of the violence of rape since the rape

of men is not an unheard of phenomenon. It occurs in military barracks, out of the way spots and frequently in prisons. Susan Brownmiller[7] cites the case of an American peace demonstrator who was raped by more than forty-five prisoners in the course of two nights spent in prison in 1973 in Washington DC. Obviously, in most cases, a man prefers to keep quiet about rapes he suffers; moreover, he generally likes to think it is impossible for him to be raped by a woman. But this is not the case.

> What happened to sixteen-year-old Bobby Hitzfield from Laramie, Wyoming was close enough to rape: six girls got out of a car, ordered him to remove his clothes and, when he refused, undressed him by force; then one of them lay naked on the grass while the others forced Bobby into position on top of her; he subsequently had to make love to the other five; immediately afterwards he committed suicide out of shame.

> In a New York subway station, during a power cut, two women forced a policeman to make love to them at gunpoint. Three young women members of a San Francisco gang threw themselves on Henry Gellert, a married man, in his shop; threatening him with knives, they undressed him and aroused him with caresses; then, under threat of castration, he had to participate in various sexual acts with them.[8]

The rape of man occurs in other societies. Bronislaw Malinowski describes *yausa*, a custom practised on the southern islands of the Trobriand archipelago, which illustrates in detail how a man can be raped by women:

> If they perceive a stranger, a man from any village but their own, passing within sight, they have the customary right to attack him, a right which, by all accounts, they exercise with zeal and energy.
>   The man is the fair game of the woman for all that sexual violence, obscene cruelty, filthy pollution

and rough handling can do to him. Thus first they pull off and tear up his pubic leaf, the protection of his modesty, and, to a native, the symbol of his manly dignity. Then, by masturbatory practices and exhibitionism, they try to produce an erection in their victim, and, when their manoeuvres have brought about the desired result, one of them squats over him and inserts his penis into her vagina. After the first ejaculation, he may be treated in the same way by another woman. Worse things are to follow. Some of the women will defecate and micturate all over his body, paying special attention to his face, which they pollute as thoroughly as they can. A man will vomit and vomit and vomit said a sympathetic informer.[9]

Rather than admit the reality of rape, man generally prefers to believe that it is impossible for him to be raped by a woman. Thus, he can amuse himself by imagining his own rape by the woman he chooses, when and how he chooses; no doubt he is less comfortable when reality chooses to catch up with him, when a razor blade threatens his testicles and he must either get a hard-on or be attacked in a deserted spot in the suburbs. Obviously, it is relatively easy for him to repress the distress which the possibility of such an event causes him, as there is little risk that he will be forced into being sexually used, and, likewise, he can easily choose not to realise that this danger hangs permanently over the lives of all women, whatever their age and physical appearance.

In most cases rape seems to man – if he does admit that it exists – as an experience whose traumatic effect should not be exaggerated. In general it does not seem to him that being raped is a particularly unusual thing for a woman since rape is not so far removed from men's habitual sexual practice: 'Of course, I understand it's not very pleasant but what do you expect! When you have no choice, it's best to give in: after all it's just a nasty few minutes to get through . . . ' Actually, even when he does not rape, man is still obsessed with imposing his wishes and controlling the relationship; the way he makes love is an illustration of this and gives a good indication of the form his sexuality takes. Man is sexually inhibited: when he 'makes love', he does not let himself get carried away by the experience of two bodies meeting, but simply gets into 'position' and lives out his fantasies.

Conjugal rights have given birth to the 'primary Western position' or the 'missionary position', in which the man is on top of the woman, crushing her with his weight: the advantage is two-fold, the woman has no choice and it stops her from moving too much if necessary. As soon as he wishes to relieve himself, he mounts her, opens her legs so he can then hump to his heart's content; it does not usually take him very long and, his business completed, he sinks down heavily. But that is the crude version; there is also the classy lover. This one has read books and knows about eroticism. When he has it off, it is not simply a question of mere release, like going to the lavatory, but of carrying out the great ritual of Love. He also prefers the on top position since it enables him to exhibit his expertise in con-trolling the situation. He indulges in a few gymnastic move-ments and little rhythmic exercises – above, below, front, back . . . one, two, three, four, five. Then he comes back to the initial position to give the final thrust. He can see his power re-flected more clearly as his partner's body convulses under his assaults. For a change, man can suggest, the woman can get on top of him: thus he can satisfy himself without too much exer-tion, something he considers he deserves after a hard day at work.

And while he is arranging his body in precise and codified positions (the *Kama Sutra* being no doubt the most famous catalogue of this kind), man does not let his mind relax and wander: he makes it work.

One of the commonest of man's fantasies is probably that of the 'ultimate possession'. Man can pursue this as far as murder – like the king in *The Arabian Nights* who, after having his adul-terous wife beheaded, slept with a different adolescent virgin every night whom he had killed the following morning to ensure that he would remain the only one to have possessed her. But most of the time, apart from the exceptional opportunities pro-vided by war, man is content to imagine that his sperm has permanently marked the woman he has just 'made love' to, or that his penis has sufficiently battered her vagina so that it will never be the same again. Another quite common fantasy, less brutal and more mystical, is that of the erotic search for unity through man's control and woman's pleasure. It is nourished by old religious myths about the complementarity of the sexes – woman as man's 'rib' in Christianity or the yin and yang of Taoism – in which the opposing principles of femininity and masculinity become 'whole' again through sexual union, ('whole' which becomes life-generating when conception occurs). A version is developed in *Le Nouveau Désordre Amoureux* where Bruckner and Finkielkraut are in raptures over woman's 'fabulous' capacity for orgasm, whilst they preach 'cautious embrace' for man, according to the following principles: 'When orgasm is unattainable, one must resolve to steal those of others; to steal eroticism from Taoism, to steal sensual delight from woman, pleasure by theft, infringement.'

Sometimes, it happens that man wants to be taken sexually 'like a woman'; in this way he hopes to be able to experience a little of that sensuality which he considers a privilege of the female sex alone. This fantasy often reveals itself in a desire to be 'lesbian', and he likes to think it is going beyond heterosexuality and the sex difference. But in fact it is only the expression of man's traditional obsession of imposing his desires on a woman, and the extension of his incapacity for experiencing his sexuality beyond his penis and his head.

By creating a whole fantasy world, man tries to alleviate his frigidity and to enhance a situation which he only experiences vicariously or as a relation of appropriation. The sensation of lack does not generally encourage him to discover his own sexuality, instead it reinforces his compulsion to possess. Man is constantly trying to regain the beauty and sensuality which he lacks, by appropriating a woman to whom he attributes those qualities that he refuses to recognise in himself. And when, sometimes, she does not come up to his expectations, he thinks he can coach and transform her until she does; but, more often, he compensates for the gulf between fantasy and reality by simply imagining that he is having it off with someone else.

Man is alienated from his own sexuality; he only experiences pleasure through his penis and his head. His body is no more than an intermediary between the two, and he does not always know quite what to do with it. He occasionally feels frustrated by this lifeless flesh, but rather than discovering his sensuality by considering himself as a whole – where penis, body and mind make up a single indissociable entity – he tries instead to compensate mentally for what he refuses physically. He does not allow himself to be led by feelings which rise in him: he controls and channels them to prevent them from spreading and causing him to lose control of himself and the situation. He represses them so much that when he can no longer hold them in he often becomes violent. His pleasure can then take a murderous form.

Trapped between his fear of letting himself go and his use of the penis as a means of appropriation, man does not see that sexuality could be something other than a struggle for power or a means of comparison. His general attitude has little to do with love or pleasure, but much more with hatred, disgust and jealousy. And its nature is well illustrated in one of the most democratically shared sentiments among men: the fear of homosexuality.

Fearful homosexuality

Homosexuality is repressed almost everywhere in the West since it is considered 'unnatural'. But the concept of nature is an ideological one. And, in any case, if it is the 'natural' one wants, homosexuality is a natural form of contraception. Homosexuality is a form of sexuality without the slightest excuse of reproduction, and its systematic repression has always gone hand in hand with other kinds of sexual repression imposed by Christianity. Thus, in everyday language, sexuality usually means heterosexuality (signifying whatever one chooses: insemination, ejaculation or struggle) and fear of homosexuality can be translated as fear of sexuality. Indeed, why should a man feel repulsion for a penis when a woman is not supposed to; why should a woman find a vulva repugnant when a man claims to find it desirable? In fact, the logic of Christian sexual repression is elsewhere: it requires everybody to be revolted by sex organs – their own as much as other people's. The repulsion is then exorcised in the institution of hetero-sexuality. However, although it is repressed, it is still always present, and reappears at the slightest opportunity in different guises: sexual crime, dirty jokes, ascetism, petty everyday sadism – and, also, in repulsion when confronted with the un-exorcised image of one's own sex organ reflected in another person.

But the fear of homosexuality in man, even if it often breaks through in these ways, does not stop there. If it were only a matter of getting over a simple aversion, it would probably not be as frequent or intense as it is: in fact it is more deeply rooted. For homosexuality itself is not just a relation between indivi-duals of the same biological sex, it is also sexuality outside the traditional relation of man–woman appropriation.

Homosexuality directly threatens man's power, as it excludes him when it is between women, and when it is between men it represents the risk for him of being sexually appropriated. He is not inordinately put out by lesbianism, he often creates a reassuring image of it which pervades his fantasies – 'It's so beautiful to see two women together!' – and when he is tired of being a voyeur, or it does not satisfy him, he knows he can always retrieve his power through insult, derision or rape. On the other hand, the possibility of being used as a sexual object by a man usually causes him great anxiety.

It is not masculine homosexuality in itself that frightens man, but a certain type of homosexuality. In its so-called 'active' form, it does not necessarily make him feel ill at ease: it does not go against his usual values – he may even find it more excit-ing to dominate a man rather than a woman. Active homo-sexuality has a long history of legitimation: it flourishes in mili-tary uniform or in other spheres of triumphant virility. It is hardly necessary to mention the ancient warriors – Persian or Greek, for example – who frequently raped their defeated enemy. One only needs to open a pornographic magazine for homosexuals to illustrate the same point: the photos often show extremely virile men, with virile 'props' – officer's helmet, thick leather, muscles, chains, threatening members, etc.

In everyday language, the homosexual is not really the man who has sexual intercourse with another man, but rather he who is supposed to be passive: the 'queen', the 'poof', the 'fairy' . . . in short, a woman. Whereas man can consider homosexuality in its 'active' form as a means of asserting his power, in its 'passive' form it is, on the contrary, a symbol of humiliation. As is often the case, words speak for themselves: man does not 'get fucked', he 'fucks'.

He wants to maintain control over himself, and the image he has of 'passive' homosexuality symbolises the loss of his powers. To 'get stuffed' is to be had, to no longer be a man, to be passive in the face of circumstances and his own pleasure, not to dominate the situation but to submit to it. The very use of the terms 'active' and 'passive' to define homosexuality (and sexual behaviour in general) reveals how sexuality is seen as a struggle; for, outside the context of a power struggle, activities such as 'penetrate' or 'be penetrated' are both as passive or active as each other, and pleasure itself is neither active nor passive, it simply flowers when given a chance.

Man's fear of homosexuality is the expression of his fear of sexuality and his wish to dominate through sex. He does not consider his penis as an organ associated with pleasure, but as an instrument of power and appropriation. And so often he is afraid that the weapon will be used against him. When confronted with a woman's vulva he generally feels a certain sense of security, as he sees himself as the only one who is armed: in reality he is more afraid of the possibility of defensive reaction from the vulva. Legends of toothed vaginas abound on all continents, and in certain societies it is frequent for the husband to be afraid of 'deflowering' his bride himself; but whatever his fears may be, man generally succeeds in getting round them, and it is rare for them to prevent him from appropriating a woman.

As a rule, man manages to repress his fear of the castrating vagina rather well, and he does his best not to imagine it as an organ of appropriation; in the same way that he refuses to believe it possible for him to be raped by a woman, he also likes to think that she cannot use him sexually. Besides, although he complains loudly that women never make the first move, as soon as a woman does express her desires and take the initiative, he usually shies away. The mere hint of that possibility can disturb him. Thus, for example, Liliana Cavani's film *Night Porter* was banned in Italy for the following reasons: 'Obscenity, scenes of excessive vulgarity showing sexual intercourse, depravity. This film, doubly pernicious as it was directed by a woman, shows a disgraceful scene in which the woman takes the initiative in a sexual relationship.'[10]

Man does not generally like to think that a woman can use him as she pleases, like a violin or a urinal: he prefers to imagine that only man can make another human being into a sexual object. It is revealing that man's fear of sexuality is often combined with his fear of homosexuality. In fact, man clearly expresses, through his revulsion for 'passive' homosexuality, his loathing for woman, as he would not like to take her place. He also reveals that he is aware of the oppressiveness of his own sexual attitude by making it clear that he would not want a sexual relationship with someone like himself.

When he is in the presence of homosexuals, the man who is not one himself, generally feels uncomfortable: he is worried and confused when he comes into contact with a world in which roles do not appear to be socially rigid, and seem likely to develop according to an individual balance of power. His reactions vary depending on appearances: in the face of a 'feminine'-looking homosexual, he may feel threatened by the image of a man who is not a real man, and this aversion to the representation of what he himself could be sometimes manifests itself in a need to beat up a 'poof' or a desire to screw him, to 'let him have it'. On the other hand, with a homosexual who looks 'virile' he may have a vague fear of ending up in his arms against his will: he is afraid of being picked up or even raped, for, in this respect, man knows he is not in the habit of letting the object of his desire have any say in the matter. He experiences, on a small scale and for a short period of time, what a woman permanently lives through; but he has the security of belonging to the man class and the reassurance of knowing that the situation will not last, that it is only a hiatus in a sex life which he experiences as the assertion of his power.

Beyond fear, masculine homosexuality is not necessarily what man imagines it to be. In itself it is obviously not the transcendance of heterosexuality and the 'man' category, nor even of sexual fear. It can just as easily be the reproduction among men of sexuality-appropriation, or the expression of distress when faced with a woman's body, or the manifestation of man's old dream of a world without women. In this sense it sometimes appears as the valorisation of virile ideas of rationality, strength or violence; and it was found as often among the Athenian philosophers and the Spartan warriors as amongst Ernst Röhm's assault squads. And yet homosexuality can also be an opportunity for a man to get to know and love himself through the love and the discovery of another man: a path to retrieving his sexuality, and to realising that pleasure is not born from the difference between the sexes, but from sex itself and the difference between individuals.

If it were not for the social division of human beings into sexes, the terms heterosexuality and homosexuality would lose their meanings; each person would be able to freely experience richer and more varied relationships than those confined within the difference between the sexes. At present, not only do they both have a meaning, but, in addition, sexuality itself, locked inside the categories 'man' and 'woman', generally does not have much to do with voluptuousness. When man pronounces such words as pleasure, love and fulfilment, he should really be saying revulsion, hatred and violence. Hanging on to the notion that his penis is an instrument of power and to his perception of the sex act as a relationship of appropriation, he struggles to find fulfilment but usually does nothing more than flounder: he only experiences emotional intensity through either inflicting or undergoing violence, and, in most cases, he experiences a frigidity which is all the more serious because he does not even know that he is frigid.

5. The myth of the phallic orgasm

Man's problem in relation to his sexuality is not how to feel pleasure, but how to fulfil his desires; and likewise, in the complementarity of the sexes, woman is not supposed to have any desire but is expected to feel pleasure. This traditional imagery has hardly been modified in the last twenty years – on the contrary, it has been revitalised by the liberalisation of the social expression of men's sexual fantasies, and by the increasingly frequent and sexualised use of the woman's body. The illusion of complementarity has also been reinforced and has found a more 'scientific' ideological endorsement thanks to medicine, which has gained a new speciality: sexology.

Whereas until the beginning of the twentieth century medical science described, in anatomy and physiology handbooks, the genital organs as being associated only with reproduction, it now takes into account certain aspects of sexual pleasure, and gives a new life to the old patriarchal myths. Beneath its permissive appearance, modern sexology in fact reproduces the most traditional ideology: it hardly recognises woman's desires beyond a 'wish to get laid' (it simply 'grants' it to her a little more often than before), and it totally ignores male sexual pleasure.

This becomes clear from the description of sexual problems. Woman's problem is presented as the absence of pleasure – frigidity; and man's as the inability to gratify his desires – impotence. Before we even start we are back to square one: complementarity is re-introduced in the definition of malfunction. In fact, if we insist on studying sexual problems from this angle, they are actually completely reversed: woman is all the more impotent because her impotence is unrecognised, and man is all the more frigid because his frigidity is ignored.

Woman's impotence is physiologically comparable to man's. The vagina may not moisten or swell, or may only do so with difficulty. Just like the penis, the vagina is not in a permanent state of excitement. Woman is no more ready to make love at any hour of day or night than man – but she is generally considered to be so. Her impotence is traditionally ignored; and she is usually 'treated' with vaseline, butter or saliva, and more or less by force. Modern sexologists have not let tradition down; for example, Masters and Johnson assert:

> If anatomical anomalies such as vaginal agenesis or an imperforate hymen are exempted and the psychological disfunction of vaginismus is discounted, it could be said provocatively that there has never been an impotent woman. Woman need only make herself available to accomplish coital connection or even to propagate the race. Legions of women conceive and raise families without ever experiencing orgasm and carry coition to the point of male ejaculation with little physical effort and no personal, reactive involvement. During coition woman has only to lie still to be physically potent. While this role of total passivity is no longer an acceptable psychological approach to sexual encounter in view of current cultural demand for active female participation, it is still an irrevocable physiological fact that woman need only lie still to be potent.[1]

It is difficult to see what concept is no longer an acceptable psychological approach when medical science considers it an 'irrevocable' fact that woman expresses her desire physiologically the minute she is on her back . . .

Man: impotent or frigid?

Sexologists generally disguise the logic underlying their theories by playing on words: in this way they associate what they call vaginal 'lubrication' difficulties with frigidity (which is often given the more medical name of 'orgasmic malfunction'). But why 'lubricate' if one does not anticipate any pleasure in being penetrated? The lack of logic is apparent. The sexologists do not define the same problem in man, the difficulty in having an erection, as also being frigidity (or an orgasmic malfunction): they call it 'impotence'. And yet the term frigidity would be much more appropriate to describe the male sexual problem. Always running after his 'potency', man thinks so little of his pleasure that, whatever happens to his penis, he often misses out completely on his own orgasm. As the writer Christiane Rochefort eloquently states: 'It is he who, at the end of the day, is frigid, and not in imagination: ejaculation without orgasm is not unusual in his little secret garden.'[2]

Sexologists take great interest in woman's potential for orgasm, but they do not even imagine that man may also experience pleasure in sexuality. To them, everything is simple: just as woman needs only to lie down in order to feel desire, man only needs to ejaculate to experience pleasure.

Modern sexology assimilates ejaculation and sexual pleasure in man to the extent that it considers ejaculation as a synonym for the male orgasm. This claim, on which most contemporary sexologists base their research, has already been questioned in scientific circles. For example, at the beginning of the fifties, the Kinsey Report noted: 'Because ejaculation is almost invariably and immediately associated with orgasm, it is often considered as the orgasm of the male. This interpretation is not acceptable.' Earlier, Wilhelm Reich, who certainly did not take existing ideas for granted, did not accept the traditional equation of ejaculation and orgasm:

> The more exactly I had my patients describe their behavior and sensations in the sexual act, the firmer became my clinical conviction that all of them, *without exception*, suffered from a *severe* disturbance of genitality. This was especially true of those men who bragged the loudest about their sexual conquests and about how many times a night they 'could do it'. There was no doubt: they were erectively very potent, but ejaculation was accompanied by little or no pleasure, or even the opposite, by disgust and unpleasant sensations . . . To the so-called potent

man, the act had the significance of conquering, piercing or raping the woman. They wanted to give proof of their potency, or to be admired for their erective endurance. This 'potency' could easily be destroyed by laying bare its motives. It served to cover up serious disturbances of erection of ejaculation. In *none* of these cases was there as much as a trace of *involuntary behavior* or *loss of alertness* during the act.[3]

In spite of these earlier attempts to understand men's sexuality, science has still taken a giant step backwards in the last few years: it has in fact re-established the old myth that ejaculation equals orgasm, even though it does not carry much weight in everyday experience.

Ejaculation in itself has little to do with sensual pleasure: it is primarily an image which concretises man's power, and a means of reproducing himself through his descendants. It is no more than the means by which he participates in procreation, but he still attributes a disproportionate importance to its role. He sometimes likes to imagine that his sperm is the seed from which life will be created, and that woman is no more than fertile soil in which to sow it. He may even wish to conserve it, and he will force himself not to spill his 'vital substance' outside himself too much. But most of the time, man does not associate ejaculation with reproduction; it is more common for him to feel that it is the culmination of his 'pleasure'. In the extension of his penis used as a weapon and instrument of appropriation, it easily becomes the shot aimed at the target, or the mark with which the owner brands the flesh of the appropriated.

And so, if ejaculation can be directly associated with pleasure, it is only in so far as it is bound up with power: outside a power relation, it has very little to do with sensuality. For if it does actually occur when the body trembles in ecstasy, it is then only a secondary sensation, and it can equally be triggered off in a man who will not let himself go the tiniest bit and experience pleasure.

Ejaculation is sometimes a semblance of orgasm but rarely its reality. But man does not often bother with such subtleties: he would rather consider his sexuality a simple matter. So, when he desires, his penis speaks for him; when he comes, his penis spits for him: he does not generally feel there is much more to it . . . were it, not for the fact that the instrument sometimes fails, and that it does not always function as expected.

Today, sexuality has its mechanics, who, before starting out on hasty repairs, have applied themselves first to defining the tool's good working order. And so they describe man's 'normal' heterosexuality as being the capacity to ejaculate and at the same time to give the woman an orgasm with the erect penis (unless of course the woman suffers from 'orgasmic malfunction'). From this simple definition 'naturally' follows the list of malfunctions, i.e. absence of ejaculation, premature ejaculation, difficulties with, or absence of, erection.

Once the problems have been so well classified, all the sexologists have to do is treat them, so that the man will be able to ejaculate again and the woman at last have an orgasm. Masters and Johnson, just to mention the pioneers, took on, between 1959 and 1970, 448 patients of the male sex and got them back in working order after a cure lasting only two weeks, and with an immediate failure rate of no more than 16.9 per cent. It is no doubt an excellent result, which has even been surpassed since in their therapy centre in St Louis, or in the numerous centres of the same kind which have been set up, during the last twenty years, primarily in the United States. But it would still be interesting to analyse what 'healthy' sexuality in man, as it is defined by sexology, conceals.

Male sexuality and its breakdowns

Man is afraid of letting himself go. He does not abandon himself to his pleasure; he confines it within the limits of his penis, and generally seeks it in his mind and on a woman's body. In this way he lives out fantasies or experiences orgasm vicariously, but he rarely lets himself be carried away by his own sensuality. He centres it on his penis without feeling that his whole body is totally sexualised: he stems the tide of pleasure at its source for fear it may submerge him if allowed to swell.

When he embraces a woman, man does not feel enveloped and overwhelmed by pleasure. He penetrates and appropriates her, projecting himself into her as if he hoped to draw from her the sensuality which he is reluctant to experience. His mind fixed on the objective, the erect penis aimed at the target, he does not allow himself to be caught up in the experience of two bodies discovering each other; he is afraid of losing his way, and prefers to follow the route already mapped out in his head. He sometimes makes an effort to satisfy his partner, and compensate for what he is missing by being a spectator of her ecstasy, but, most of the time, while he ejaculates, he is content to reel off in his mind the mental film in which he finds all the images of the sensations he lacks. Man fragments himself, his desexualised body jerks between his penis and his head. He deliberately alienates himself from his pleasure, he does not feel completely involved in sensuality; he nips the storm in the bud for fear of drowning, his ecstasy then becomes mere wavelets: four thrusts of the pelvis, a few drops of sperm and it is all over.

Man habitually compensates for his sexual dissatisfaction through various forms of mental and material satisfaction. The advantages which can be gained from the sexual appropriation of a woman are indeed many and varied – from the satisfaction of having lived out his fantasy to the possibility, once the 'act' is over, of having his meals cooked or his buttons sewn on. However, it can also happen that man's sexual frustration can take a pathological form: satyriasis.

The word 'satyriasis' is rarely used, and yet it defines a classic masculine sexual disorder: 'An abnormally intense and persistant desire in a man for sexual intercourse' (*Collins English Dictionary*, 1979). In fact, it is the equivalent of 'nymphomania' – 'An abnormally intense and persistent desire in a woman for sexual intercourse' (*ibid.*) The term 'nymphomaniac' has even entered everyday vocabulary, where it often replaces 'bitch' or 'whore'; it sounds undeniably more elegant, and offers a little scientific endorsement to the speaker. What is more, satyriasis and nymphomania express two comparable disorders, which manifest themselves in a condition of permanent excitement which can never be satisfied: 'In the case of satyriasis and nymphomania, sexual excitation does not subside.'[4]

In other words, the man suffering from satyriasis runs indefatigably after any sexual relationship in the hope of finding satisfaction, but always remains as frustrated as he was before. In fact, satyriasis is far more common than nymphomania. It can be found, in more or less pathological forms, in places as diverse as the conjugal bed, the adulterer's chamber, the doorway of the brothel, the corner of a dark street, the seats of a smoky nightclub – and, whatever the 'score' chalked up, and subsequently bragged about, the man will still be as sexually unfulfilled as before.

Man's 'normal' sexuality does not usually have much to do with fulfilment: it is the screen in the fight man has with his penis. The struggle is sometimes fierce, and the outcome is never certain as the spectre of impotence is a permanent threat. If one understands words in the context of prevailing ideas, their meaning becomes clear: erection is not a delicate warmth which spreads from the penis through the rest of the body, nor a pleasant swelling of the penis when the senses are receptive to voluptuousness. Man decides otherwise: erection is the symbol of his power, the assertion of his potency, and its absence is simply his impotence. He makes his penis what it is not, he tries to control it and will not allow it to function to its own rhythm, and he is astonished when it sometimes plays dirty tricks on him.

Man's pleasure usually has so little to do with sexuality itself that it would not be too exaggerated to consider his lack of erection, his 'impotence', as his normal sexual state. Reich, wondering how his patients imagined their pleasure, in particular when masturbating, was struck by the discovery that:

> *Not in a single patient was the act of masturbation accompanied by the phantasy of experiencing pleasure in the normal sexual act.* At best, the phantasy was that they 'were having sexual intercourse'. On closer investigation, it turned out that the patients neither visualised nor felt anything concrete in this phantasy. This expression of 'having sexual intercourse' was used mechanically; in most

cases, it covered the desire to 'prove oneself a man',
to rest in the arms of a woman (usually of an older
woman), or to 'penetrate a woman'. In brief, it might
mean anything except genital sexual pleasure.[5]

Why get a hard-on if one does not anticipate any pleasure at the
thought of penetration? Masculine logic does not usually function in this way; in most cases the question does not even arise,
and anyway the answer is elsewhere. When man can't get a
hard-on he must try to, come hell or high water, and if he cannot, he is not a man any more, not a real one. 'Impotence'
easily becomes an obsession which haunts him and an anxiety
which gnaws at him – he sometimes screws to the rhythm of 'will
get it up – won't get it up' – as he is never really sure if his tool
is in good working order. Under guarantee or not, it can desert
him at any time and leave him in the lurch just when he most
needs it. As the writer and critic Jean Freustié said on a television programme on sexuality, man's fear is 'facing an obstacle
without the means to climb over it'.[6] In that case, what can be
done? The question is ominous, and the reply often proves
worrying:

> Mr Gilbert Peters, 41, a foreman from Metz, on a trip to
> Paris, was feeling erotic. He let himself be tempted by the
> songs of the sirens who haunt the thickets of the Bois de
> Boulogne. One of them, answering to the misnomer
> Martine Pucelle ['Pucelle' means 'virgin' in French] agreed
> to keep him company. Was it the atmosphere of the place
> or simply emotion? Peters was unable to fulfil his contract.
> His ego would not have suffered if he had not noticed that
> his failure had been watched by several witnesses. In
> a fury he prepared to spray tear gas at the voyeurs, who
> were already roaring with laughter. He then grabbed his
> knife and set off in pursuit. The managing director of a
> large Parisian company, who was passing by, got the blade
> in his buttocks. (*France-Soir*, 4 July 1974)

Through wanting to hoist the flag at all costs, man sometimes
loses his erection; then he spends his time running after it, but

he usually runs in the wrong direction. He does not see that his broken-down penis is attuned to his sexuality; he presses on it like a biceps muscle to try and make it swell. He does not attempt to accept himself as he is, and let himself be carried away discovering the hidden pleasures of his body: on the contrary, he turns to fantasies, hoping to recover his proud hard-on as fast as possible.

Sometimes he manages it, sometimes he does not. But even if he is successful, he will always remain worried: the thought of humiliation will dog him until old age releases him from the fatigue of having to get it up. Unfortunately for him, the age at which he can escape from his self-imposed obligation has still not been clearly determined. Man still does not know exactly, when, without the risk of letting the side down, he may cease to struggle to produce an erection on demand. As for real pleasure in this long race for erection, it is out of the question; but what does it matter, as potency *is* man's pleasure?

A new fear has now been added to man's fear of 'impotence', and that is premature ejaculation: nowadays it is not enough to have a hard-on to be a man, it must be one that is maintained for a long time. Until recently, man did not consider rapid ejaculation to be a serious sexual problem. As long as he could ratify his appropriation by performing a few movements inside the vagina, the business was done and the contract fulfilled. Rapid ejaculation enabled him not to linger – he was sometimes even proud of his 'quickie' – it gave an undeniable advantage in his attempts to improve the hypothetical record in the love marathon. Moreover, his wife did not usually complain, she could extricate herself faster, and, as for the prostitute, it suited her wish to speed up the flow of customers. But for twenty years or so, premature ejaculation has been put alongside 'impotence' in the ranking of serious male sexual disorders. The sexologists have now realised that it does not enable man to fulfil the new contract of modern heterosexuality: the woman's orgasm.

If one listens to some of them, one might think that premature ejaculation was a feminine problem. Masters and Johnson, for example, give the following definition: 'The Foundation considers a man a premature ejaculator if he cannot control his ejaculatory process for a sufficient length of time during intra-vaginal containment to satisfy his partner in at least 50 per cent of their coital connections.' But they add: 'If the female partner is persistently nonorgasmic for reasons other than the rapidity of the male's ejaculatory process, there is no validity to the defi-nition.'[7]

Dr Reuben provides a definition along the same lines; it is developed by his patient Nathalie, who talks about her relation-ship with Jack:

> I just don't know what to say! He tells me it's my fault but I'm willing to do anything! I just don't know what to do. I'm tired of crying! It doesn't do any good any more! It's the same every time. We go to bed, Jack says he'll be great this time. He plays with me long enough to get me all excited. And then he goes to put it in. As soon as his organ touches me, he comes right away. It's driving me crazy! The worst thing is his smile! At least he can look disappointed. It's almost as if he's doing it on purpose.

A psychiatrist as brilliant as Dr Reuben cannot leave his patient in such a state of shock; and, at the same time, he is going to enlighten his millions of readers, who hope to find out once and for all 'everything about sex':

> Nathalie put her finger on it that time. Jack is doing it on purpose. Only he doesn't realise it. He expresses his resentment of Nathalie eloquently with his phallus. The results are hard on her but easy on him. He has regular and frequent intercourse, with an orgasm every time. Nathalie hasn't had an orgasm (except when she masturbates) for almost ten years. The smile is characteristic of men with premature ejaculations – they are all profusely apologetic, but their regrets have a hollow ring.[8]

To the sexologist's way of thinking, premature ejaculation does not mar man's pleasure, except, of course, through his disappointment in not satisfying the woman. Masters and Johnson are categorical: 'It is evident that man's sexual inadequacy is not related directly to his ability or inability to attain orgasmic release of sexual tensions. Psychosocial influences certainly create clinical states of male sexual inadequacy, but rarely are they directed specifically toward the orgasmic experience.'[9] This is hardly surprising, given the confusion of ejaculation with male orgasm: what does it matter when or how it comes, as long as it comes! All the same, it is surprising and somewhat disconcerting that men like Reuben and Masters, have such a limited knowledge of their own bodies: either they have never had an orgasm, or they have never had a premature ejaculation; but in any case, they should be better informed, for, whatever they may say, the man who ejaculates rapidly rarely achieves orgasm.

Premature ejaculation is, in fact, a common form of male frigidity, and is easy to define once it is described with reference to man: it is simply premature in relation to the development of his pleasure. Reich depicted this with a curve: at the beginning, over-excitement, then a slight protrusion of pleasure corresponding to ejaculation, and finally descent through displeasure back to neutrality. Even if one has never experienced it directly nor through a lover, it is fairly easy to imagine what happens to the body during premature ejaculation: the mind crammed with fantasies and fears, man is sometimes so tense and over-excited that he can no longer control the restricted area to which he confines his sexuality. Mind and penis levelled at the target, he does not let the sexual energy spread through his body, and at the first contact with the moistness of the vagina, it soon overflows: the energy is released in the ejaculatory reflex. A few little convulsions shake the hips and it is quickly over; man has only to fall asleep or apologise.

Man does not generally feel premature ejaculation as his own non-satisfaction, he usually realises that it is a problem through his partner's frustration. He does not try to relax to enable pleasure to be diffused through his body, on the contrary he endeavours to exert an even more stringent control over himself. So, the traditional 'cures' concentrate on everything that can desensitise the penis, and chase erotic fantasies from the mind: they include the use of anaesthetising creams, the consumption of tranquillisers, the practice of masturbation before the 'act' and diverse attempts at thinking of 'something else' – counting sheep, mentally leafing through the telephone directory, imagining an unpleasant situation. Once again there is not much room for pleasure.

Sexology, however, has made all these botch-jobs look rather primitive. The victory over premature ejaculation is one of their greatest successes. Masters and Johnson claim a very low failure rate which includes relapses during the five-year ' probation period'. This miracle-cure is based on the 'squeeze technique' carried out by the woman (who squeezes the coronal ridge of the penis between her thumb, forefinger and middle finger): fairly strong pressure enables impending ejaculation to be checked and kept back. Using this method, alternating a cycle of compression and masturbation, and then another of compression and penetration (the whole procedure being carried out in particular positions and to a precise rhythm), within a fortnight the man finally succeeds in acquiring a completely fresh ability to control his ejaculation. All the same, he must take good care of it as he is warned: 'It is also important to emphasise that if circumstances lead to separation of marital unit members for a matter of several weeks, coital exposure after the marital unit is physically reunited may find the male returning to his role as a premature ejaculator.' But he is not left to fend alone: 'Obviously the procedure in this situation is to re-employ the squeeze technique for several consecutive coital exposures. If constituted with warmth and understanding, ejaculatory control will return rapidly.'[10]

It is only within the area to which man limits his sexuality that the sex mechanics apply themselves to tightening up the bolts. They refuse to see that what is needed is to smash the dams which hold back his pleasure, so that it can course through his whole body. Man's sexual problem, whether it is expressed through premature ejaculation or absence of erection is not lack of control over himself, but, on the contrary, the inability to let himself be carried away by voluptuousness.

This atrophied sexuality is sometimes exacerbated in the absence of ejaculation: 'Not only does he fail to ejaculate, he never reaches orgasm. It is the male equivalent of female frigidity. The erection stays rigid, sensation is more or less intact, (except for soreness after the first hour) but for the man there is no end.'[11] Doctor Reuben thinks he can limit male frigidity to this relatively rare disorder which is, in fact, only one example. Absence of ejaculation can even be considered as the summit of male sexuality: the man who does not ejaculate is in reality keeping perfect control over himself; he is not making even the slightest concession to nature. He carefully keeps his 'vital substance' inside him, and he rises above the demands of the flesh by exerting total control over his body. At the same time, he makes his partner crave sex like an animal, so that he can relish his triumph over woman's lust and fuck her till she drops.

Absence of ejaculation, prolonging the erection indefinitely, is a common masculine fantasy, but it is rarely achieved. It is in fact difficult to attain; what is more, if it has it glories and joys, it also brings its miseries and woes, and man generally prefers to end up with relief.

Man obviously is not doomed to this frigidity which undermines him and makes him dominate, rape and murder. Stifled by his mind and crammed into his penis, his sexuality wants to spread: his body, which he controls and desensitises to send it to be destroyed in the struggles for power, is only waiting for the control to slacken so that it can live. Sensual pleasure is no more a female prerogative than power is a male privilege. Outside of social categories, everybody is unique, and can freely develop their potential which is crippled by being confined inside the sex difference. If only he would get rid of his obsession with appropriation and sacrosanct penetration, a man could venture into a sexual world where all caresses are possible, and where each person's ecstasy is unpredictable as they allow themselves to be guided only by pleasure and the sensation of oneness with the pleasure of the other.

6. The daddy and the rapist

The separation of humans into two groups according to the anatomy of their sex organs, expresses in itself the appropriation of the woman group by the man group, and this generalised appropriation enables each man to take a woman for his particular use. This relation, where one class is owned by another, is not only legalised in the marriage contract and institutionalised in prostitution, it determines all relations between men and women: every man is the potential owner of every woman. If he cannot ask for, buy or hire her, he can always rape her, and even if he gives up his rights, he can still avail himself of them again whenever he chooses. Whatever his attitude and feelings about the appropriation of women, he remains, within patriarchy, 'a man', and even if he decides not to take advantage of the prerogatives attached to his category, they are still socially established as his. But most of the time, man does not even ask himself this sort of question. He is content simply to enjoy his privileges, and his behaviour as owner oscillates between two extremes: he is either the daddy or the rapist.

The daddy is the reassuring side of the phallus, the one which protects, nourishes and judges; in other words, appropriation through protection, providing the means of subsistence and deciding what a 'woman' is or is not. Man is fond of this daddy uniform and often likes to imagine that it is he who makes a woman feel secure – 'Don't worry darling, I'm here.' He thinks he is as solid as a rock, ready to run any risk to protect a creature he imagines to be fragile and defenceless. He is the knight in shining armour carrying off the peasant girl in rags, away from her woes, he is the rescuer of Sleeping Beauty from the enchanted forest who snatches the defenceless girl from the clutches of the wicked.

Man often takes a malicious delight, in his fantasies, in putting women in desperate predicaments, so that, having saved their lives, he can subsequently appropriate them in triumph. And so, from fairy tales to James Bond, including adolescent dreams, the tradition is perpetuated by being honoured. And the reality of everyday life is hardly any different: the collective appropriation of women means that any woman who has not been already clearly taken is available for a man to appropriate at any moment. That is, she is constantly threatened – physically as well – with appropriation (until it occurs, when she is granted a relative respite). Seeing the situation in a more individual light, one could say that, like the mafioso who instigates a rule of terror in order to justify his racket, man creates a reign of fear to enable him to protect: he rapes the others to be daddy to one – moreover, does he not make the distinction himself between the women he 'screws' and the woman he marries?

Once a woman has been exclusively appropriated, man guarantees his 'protection' but retains the threat that he might withdraw it, at the same time making himself necessary and trying to treat 'his' woman as a child. This process is part of a global ideology according to which a woman is not supposed to be capable of looking after herself. We can see it expressed in a range of activities from filling in a tax form, which she is considered incapable of doing by herself, or mending a fuse, which she is not supposed to know about, to driving a car, which she is bound to crash into a brick wall. That man himself may skid on a wet road, or not know the different between 13 and 15 amps or has not got a clue about tax law, makes no difference. It is enough that Alan Jones, Thomas Edison and the Chancellor of the Exchequer are men, for any man to feel that driving, electricity and the tax system are biologically impregnated in him. Woman should not have to be told twice and should be happy among her pots and pans in the kitchen – 'Don't touch that! I'm coming!' He is a man, *therefore* he knows and he acts.

Of course, given the rate at which traditional values are losing credibility nowadays, man's image as the all-powerful protector has become somewhat tarnished. But even so, it still holds sway: the saviours and supermen remain high in the charts of men's fantasies, and the medieval knights have simply been transformed into crusaders of domestic cleanliness. The procedure remains exactly the same: man 'proves' his love by overcoming difficulties, woman shows her gratitude by placing herself entirely at his disposal; he proudly invents washing powder, and she does the washing.

Man does not acquire a woman only by 'protecting' her, he also provides for her. Daddy is generous, he feeds and houses; but underneath this magnanimous exterior – which he sometimes emphasises – he is, in reality, concealing his attempts to prevent a woman surviving unless she serves him. Indeed, whether in the guise of father, husband, boss or lover, man generally does his best to discourage a woman from working for a salary – if she insists, or if the couple need the money, it will only be as a secondary income. She thus becomes more dependent on him or on another member of the man class, to provide for her vital needs.

The means and the arguments used, individually as well as collectively, to keep women out of the labour market, are many and varied. One of the principal methods of dissuasion is, of course, to limit the salary that a woman can hope to earn by working, so that man can declare 'It's not worth a woman's while to go out to work!' What is more, he generally backs up his reasoning with the traditional 'Woman's place is in the home' or the trendier 'Wage-earning's a load of shit; you're not going to fall for it, are you?' And when these arguments are on the wane their supporters in government resort to chanting the old adage about woman returning to the home.

Authority

It is as a class that men, in order to maintain woman's financial dependence, attempt to restrict her access to the labour market. In 'Capitalism, Patriarchy and Job Segregation by Sex',[1] Heidi Hartman shows, for example, how male workers in England and America coped with the threat the development of capitalism represented to male workers' power over women. She traces the crucial role they played, through their unions, in restricting women's participation in wage labour which could have provided them a base for material independence. Since then, in the West, the situation has settled down. Capitalism is so well integrated into patriarchy that it sometimes manages to disguise its existence; and the contradiction between the interests of men in general and those of capitalists in particular have mostly been resolved by giving women lower salaries, a double working-day and barring them from or allowing them only limited access to many professions.

At present, in the middle of the economic crisis, two opposing tendencies are developing: on the one hand, women are worse hit by unemployment, and exhortations to keep them at home or send them back there are becoming increasingly strident; but on the other, their underpaid work is an incitement to employ them in order to keep the cost of wages down. And so many traditionally masculine professions are being feminised as soon as the wages offered become 'feminine' – on condition, of course, that the prestige attached to the job is not too high. The most recent and striking example comes from the United States where the rate of pay for an ordinary soldier in the armed forces has fallen so low that the job is beginning to lose its exclusively male character:

> To compensate for the shortage of manpower, the army is recruiting more and more women: nearly sixty thousand at present, of whom 39 per cent are assigned to the traditional auxiliary positions as office workers, medical assistants etc. But there are increasing numbers of women occupying the more qualified positions which, in the past, were reserved for men: air or land transport, technical maintenance etc. Also it is increasingly common for them to receive training for combat, but in their contract it is still stipulated that they cannot be recruited to fight.' (*Le Monde*, 17 October 1980)

Unable to sell their labour power, or to get a good enough price for it, women are often driven to selling themselves: to 'giving' themselves to a man. Once again, the words speak for themselves; in marriage or in 'love', it is no longer only the woman's labour power which is at stake, but woman herself who is appropriated in her entirety – as Collette Guillaumin puts it: 'It is the material unit which produces the labour power that is taken in hand.'[2]

In the marriage contract, or the tacit convention which 'love' is, there is no limit to the work-time which the woman owes her husband or lover. 'For a woman . . . to love is to relinquish everything for the benefit of a master,'[3] observed Simone de Beauvoir. According to Pope Paul VI: 'Woman is the companion, the partner, the mysterious source of life . . . for her, the customary heroism of sacrifice.'[4] Man can go out and confront the dangers and challenges of the world, since he knows that when he comes back, he can put his feet up and read his newspaper in peace, changing the world in his imagination while his wife finishes the washing-up and cleans the kitchen. In one way or another, man collects the medals and the applause whilst, off stage, woman dresses his wounds, types his manuscripts, relieves his penis, feeds his stomach, keeps his house, brings up his children. She is entirely at his service and is completely eclipsed in the glow of his triumph.

In return for his supposed protection, man obtains the sacrifice of woman's own self, a sacrifice that in the name of love is, in most cases, legally ratified by the marriage vows. This relationship is reminiscent of that of feudal lord and serf in the Middle Ages: the former, in the name of divine right, 'protected' the latter from being attacked by other feudal lords, and was 'kind' enough to let the serf work for him. However, in this type of relationship, it was possible to free oneself from the power of the lord of the manor by fleeing the countryside and taking refuge in the city:

> The serf was 'part of the land'; if he could escape the land, a path to emancipation was open to him. Woman is like the land. Like certain slaves, it is she (her body) who is owned. And that is not only in marriage – the most obvious form, perhaps too obvious. In fact all women belong to each man, and each woman belongs to all men.[5]

Man does not only appropriate a woman through marriage;

in fact, he can only marry because women have already been appropriated as a class. As Collette Guillaumin comments: 'to acquire a slave "normally" *in a slave class which has already been formed*, all one has to do is *buy* one, to acquire a woman in a society where the woman class has been formed, one only has to *ask for* or *buy* her.'[6]

Daddy is not content to protect and provide; he judges and imposes his idea of what a woman must be. He is the father who helps make his daughter a woman, the husband or lover who seeks to mould his woman according to his interests and fantasies and, more globally, he is the creator of the concept 'woman' which he perpetuates, from one generation to the next, to justify the appropriation of women.

Since Pygmalion made his ideal woman out of ivory and succeeded in bringing her to life, creating a woman has been one of man's favourite pastimes. From childhood and adolescence, he starts to fashion his feminine model; he imagines the behaviour that women in general must have, and also that of 'his' woman in particular. In addition, he itemises the shape and size he prefers for each limb and external organ of their bodies – isolating them to the point where he gives certain parts their own personality: 'Ah, they're the most beautiful breasts I've ever come across,' he sometimes exclaims in ecstasy, but even so, he does not forget how his 'ideal woman' should look. He attaches great importance to her weight, her height, the texture of her skin, the colour of her eyes, the shade of her hair and even – why not? – the number of breasts: 'It is biologically conceivable to manufacture women with two pairs of breasts. This is doubtless a proposition that biology has to offer tradition,' wrote Abraham Moles in 'Open Letter to the Situationists'.[7]

However, man does not only cut women into pieces in his fantasies, he also looks for them in life as he imagines them in his head, and he tries to shape them according to the model that he has created in his mind. This attitude is particularly noticeable in the husband or lover who chooses a woman according to established standards of beauty and behaviour; once he has appropriated her he tries to make her correspond even further to his interests and fantasies. But this common attitude among men is not only to be found in individual relationships, on the contrary, it is usually stressed when man devotes himself to artistic or intellectual pursuits. In painting or music, the cinema, literature or human sciences, creating 'woman' is one of man's greatest sources of inspiration.

Art offers some men the opportunity of moulding their feminine archetypes while providing other men with the necessary images to nourish their own fantasies. Sculpture and painting have traditionally provided a fertile terrain for the expression of dreams of the 'ideal woman' (and sometimes of nightmares of 'repugnant woman'). Museums are so cluttered with examples that there is no need to go into detail here; classical statues can, however, be mentioned, since they still preserve their role as an aesthetic reference, even though they have been amputated, in part or altogether. Heads, arms or legs are missing – as if as long as the breasts and hips are there, the rest of the woman is irrelevant. Many painters, sculptors and photographers do not always wait for time to take its toll, they simply eliminate the parts of woman's body they themselves consider superfluous: thus the vagina and breasts are often isolated, as if their presence alone were enough to satisfy the creator and the spectator.

In literature and the cinema, man has even more opportunity to give free rein to his fantasies; he is not restricted to reproducing fixed attitudes, and he can precisely describe the behaviour he expects from a 'woman'. Women have a rough time of it, page after page, image after image, and the story is always near enough the same; after all conceivable adventures throughout literature and the cinema, the destiny of women is invariably death or submission, rape, prostitution or marriage.

In art, man expresses his dreams of appropriating women as well as appropriating the women of his dreams; and he achieves both in real life relationships with women all the better for having created standards of beauty and behaviour. The artistic approach reflects on all men who benefit from the social impact of prescriptive images of 'woman' in the realisation of their fantasies and the safeguarding of their interests. And the artist is not alone in proposing female models. From the height of his rostrum, the social scientist is also adept at providing canons: conscientiously he reproduces the concept 'woman' and brings it into line with his recent findings.

This activity, which consists of providing at the same time a basis and scientific justification for the appropriation of women and for the division of human beings into sexes, went on relatively unhampered until recently. Man could discuss at leisure whether or not woman had a soul, claim that the division of labour between the sexes was natural, or calmly elaborate theories on female sexuality. But since the end of the sixties, things have changed somewhat; the thinkers of the man class have had their patch trodden on by feminist theoreticians. In most cases they react with sarcasm, censorship or irony to this danger which threatens their authority, not only in their laboratories, but also in their dining rooms and beds.

Man has a soft spot for the uniform of daddy, it satisfies him in many and various ways: daddy knows and does what is best for women, and at the same time he feathers his own nest. On the material level, the activities which involve, amongst other things, creating 'woman', and making woman understand what they could be, generally also lead to an interesting combination of work conditions, remuneration and prestige. But, even when these professions – ideologist, psychoanalyst, film director, photographer, etc. – are not open to him, daddy always has the possibility of appropriating a woman to attend to his needs, those of his family and his property. On a more spiritual level, realising his fantasies in a human being gives him a great sense of satisfaction, even though his image can be disappointing: 'Oh the despair of Pygmalion, who could have created a statue and made only a woman![8]

Through the creation and possession of a personalised object or a concept, man displays the symbol of his success: 'his woman'. The connoisseur is able to recognise the artist's hallmark, or the academic a well-polished theory, and the skilled creator, the happy proprietor, is admired for his mastery and envied for his comfort. But, in spite of all the advantages, man is generally not content with the status of daddy; for he also has 'natural desires' which need satisfying, and, in any case, only his penis can truly confirm his appropriation: at this point daddy becomes rapist.

Possessing the desired object

Man does not always wear the seemingly reassuring expression of daddy. He has another less presentable side, the (badly) hidden side of the penis: his so-called 'natural desires' which will inevitably drive him to rape, or, to speak less crudely, to fuck a woman without asking her consent. In fact, his attitude has nothing much to do with nature, it serves above all to disguise the simple fact that, when he wants to use a woman for sexual purposes, man has little concern for her feelings; he only takes into consideration his own desires and apprehensions about the 'act'. If his fantasies and obsession with possession drive him to appropriate a woman, it is only his fears, his shyness, or his ethics which may hold him back and not a woman's refusal – besides, when a woman says no, is she not supposed to mean yes? When man makes a woman into the object of desire, he is often prepared to go to any lengths in order to 'possess' her sexually.

Man does not generally envisage relationships other than as power relations. He chases, approaches or seduces a woman to conquer her; the language he uses is revealing and sounds more like that of a sailor, hunter or warrior than of a lover. A woman is not a person to be discovered, but a body to be undressed; he does not really 'know' her until he has penetrated her vagina. She is a prey to be slaughtered; he sets traps for her. She is a town he draws up plans to invade; he imagines she is a fortress to be stormed by force, and, as he has a taste for combat, the more she resists, the more he insists.

An easy victory does not usually interest him much, he prefers to have to make an effort. Then he can give his talents free rein. For he has a variety of sexual gambits. He can be flamboyant, try to impress or clown around. He laughs, cries or shows his fangs. He sweats, he suffers. He sometimes goes so far as to throw himself at the feet of the desired object. But what does it matter what he does or says in front of a woman:

the most important thing is to win, to end the siege in victory and penetrate in triumph the vagina he has so craftily forced open. Once the conquest is over and the laurels won, the relationship often bores him – we have seen the poverty of his sexuality, and can understand his lack of interest in his 'onanistic coitus'. What really matters to the 'real man', is the challenge itself: the difficult appropriation of the 'inaccessible' woman, the virgin territory that he wants to conquer. When his attempts conclude in victorious penetration, there is nothing left but to boast of his success and set off to look for new targets.

Thus, man wages war on the battlefield of love, for 'the warrior loves danger and sport, that is why he loves woman: she is the most dangerous sport of all.'[9] But it sometimes happens, during these dangerous liaisons, that he gets caught at his own game, that he believes the nonsense he spouts – 'Oh my love, I'd do anything for you, I put my life in your hands,' and so on – and instead of leaving once again for battle, he may want to annex his latest conquest for good, and marry her. His sexual appropriation now takes a different form. It is no longer a question of possessing a woman once and for all through her vagina, but of using her vagina from time to time for his sexual release. Conjugal rights provide for his needs in this case and legitimate rape – a sort of permanent 'landlord's due'[10] enacted by the husband. The wife is subjected to providing a sexual service which she cannot get out of: not only must the marriage be regularly 'consummated' on pain of breach of contract but, furthermore, rape within marriage has no legal existence. If she does not submit to her husband's wishes, he can quite legally exercise his rights by force. On condition, of course, that he does not disturb the peace and that the wife does not make too much noise and wake the neighbours.

However, man does not always need violence to appropriate a woman sexually and oblige her to satisfy his desires. His repertoire as rapist is extremely varied, and he also knows how to get what he wants by taking a gentle line; here, violence only hovers in the background, or is used as a last resort. Among the catalogue of seduction techniques, certain methods find favour in his eyes. Money and status are, for example, classic means: dinner out, a drive, or a spin on a motorbike are supposed to buy a night of sex. Similarly, intellectual, sporting or artistic achievement, or a well-established career, are frequently used as a way of gaining access to a woman's vagina. But distributing crumbs of his financial success, or allowing woman to bask in his fame, are not the only means man uses when he wants a fuck: they are accompanied by promises and lies, and, more often than not, these serve to compensate for the lack of money or the insignificance of achievement.

The famous 'chatting-up technique' he is so proud of, or so sad not to possess, seems to be one of the tools necessary for carrying out his schemes. He adapts it to the situation, trying to come up to what he thinks are the expectations of the woman he covets. Man can assert the opposite of what he believes, or adopt attitudes he disapproves of, with the unique aim to please. He feels that, in any case, what he says or does with a woman is of little consequence, as long as his behaviour enables him to reach the goal he has set himself: to possess her.

Man is not content simply to avail himself of these well-known means of sexual appropriation; he usually combines them with others which are just as common. Seduction until the woman is exhausted is, for intance, one of his favourite schemes and one of his best ploys: he pesters a woman so insistently – in the street, the pub, by phone, at her home – that her patience or her strength gives out and she prefers to yield to his advances than to continue resisting them. Furthermore, this method is usually embellished with reasoning which resorts to all the ruses of patriarchal ideology, from intimidation, to a semblance of rationality – 'Oh, come on, be logical, you call yourself liberated, so why don't you want to fuck?' – to the many processes daddy uses to be able to rape without having to resort to violence.

A man does not like waiting; when he wants, the woman must want. And if, in spite of all his efforts, she still does not acquiesce, there is always (before resorting to violence) emotional blackmail: 'Be kind, go on, you can easily do that, just this once. It's not much to ask and it means so much to me . . . You know you are important to me.' Tears in his eyes, he can often get her to surrender without having to brandish his weapons. Besides, when necessary, he will unhesitatingly use both threat – 'I could force you, you know' – and compassion. The end of a letter sent to *Libération* is a good example of this traditional behaviour:

> I would like to put in an ad: '22-year-old virgin
> would like to change and meet a girl who will teach him to
> make love and bear his loneliness.' Maybe that is
> aggressive, I don't know. But if nobody answers, I'll carry
> on glaring at women until the evening I have one
> too many and perhaps I'll become a rapist. Perhaps,
> perhaps not.[11]

Man does not always bother with subterfuge to appropriate a woman sexually. He has been known to use violence as well: alone or in a crowd, he knows how to establish the law of the jungle. Flick-knife in hand or fists clenched, most of the time he manages to screw the woman he wants when he wants. Sometimes, like a true hunter, he hides in the dark and takes his quarry by surprise when the time comes; yet, to ensure his success he must know how to be patient and learn to manoeuvre. Eldridge Cleaver in *Soul on Ice*, recalls how he had to practise in the ghetto on 'black girls' before he was 'smooth enough' to cross the tracks and seek out 'white prey'. But generally the lone rapist, who is prepared to use force, prefers to come into the open and get what he wants by guile. Emmanuèle Durand describes one such traditional 'escalation' where the usual pattern develops from an obliging, 'What! At this hour . . . I'll drive you home,' or an innocent, 'Come in for just a minute, I'll show you the book I was telling you about.' Then the door closes behind him, the smile leaves his face and the mere demonstration of his brutality is generally sufficient for man to obtain what he was after:

> All that I glimpsed in a few seconds seemed more terrible
> than closing my eyes and waiting for it to be over. I neither
> wanted to die nor to bear unnecessary scars. The rape, in

any case, had already been consummated, through violence and humiliation . . . The matter took thirty seconds. A friend I was telling about the incident asked me, to my great stupefaction, if I had had an orgasm! Which seems to me to prove that he did not distinguish between rape and making love.[12]

From the use of physical coercion to all the more or less gentle seduction techniques, man has a wide range of ways of forcing a woman to allow herself to be sexually possessed. And he is so sure of the legitimacy of his power that even if he does not approach all the women he meets, he still behaves like the potential proprietor of all those he passes in the street.

Man likes to show a woman that he could appropriate her, that he can take her whenever he so wishes. He does not deny himself any opportunity to exercise his ownership rights – in the street, at work, at any gathering of family or friends. From slobbering kisses, coarse jokes and lewd insinuations, uttered in a woman's presence, to eyes which undress her and scrutinise her like meat on a stall: 'A woman's body is so beeootiful!' 'Look at those legs . . . and that wiggle, eh!' But worse, man is not content just to stare and show his appreciation noisily; often he makes no bones about groping. Wandering hands take advantage of the slightest opportunity, talking is accompanied by clammy pawing and he makes the most of rush-hour crowds to rub up against the woman next to him in the tube, preferably a woman he has selected. All in all, he imposes continuous pressure and woman's daily life is governed by sexual terrorism, constantly reminding her that she can be sexually appropriated at any moment.

The only limitation on the appropriation of a woman for sexual purposes is, in fact, not to encroach too obviously on the interests of another man – father, pimp, husband or lover. Legal practice concerning rape is, in this respect, revealing. For a woman to obtain legal recognition that she has been raped, not only must the rapist not be her husband, but, amongst other obstacles, she must submit to a gynaecological examination to establish the presence of injuries and, above all, traces of sperm. Patriarchal ideology and institutions do not generally admit that rape has taken place unless there is obvious evidence of violence and, in addition, the assault must culminate in ejaculation. This last point, which has, in itself, little to do with rape, becomes a matter of vital importance in the courts – it indicates the possibility of a pregnancy which is undesired by the victim's rightful owner: the husband or the father. In other words, the crime only really exists if it might be harmful to another man. This attitude, which is codified by law and guaranteed by tradition, explicitly reveals one of the many expressions of the collective appropriation of women. It can be found, too, in everyday relations, where every woman who has not been clearly appropriated by a man prepared to defend his rights, is considered 'available'.

A 'free' woman does not remain so for long. She represents a challenge and taking possession of her depends mainly on a balance of power between men: on a fight or an agreement between them. Matters are sometimes dealt with amicably, to the tune of 'May I borrow your daughter, Sir?' But things can sometimes take an aggressive turn: the woman then becoming the object of a fist-fight, of a verbal contest or a display of prestige and money. Men consider women as chattels – except for the obvious fact that they 'move and speak, which complicates matters considerably'.[13] So the acquisition of a woman gives rise to the usual conflicts and transactions in this sort of business. The most striking example in the history of western mythology is doubtless that of the leaders of ancient Greece who agreed that the women they judged to be the most beautiful should be given exclusively to one of them, and who had to launch their fleets – after Paris had broken the agreement – in order to honour their pact and bring Helen back to Menelaus, to whom she had been loyally assigned. The Trojan War lasted for ten years, and is still today a symbol of the discord that women are supposed to sow among men, causing even best friends to end up at loggerheads.

A woman actually has only a limited and indirect influence over the transactions that concern her. Her mere appearance amongst a group of men is enough to set in motion two types of male behaviour which are only superficially contradictory: connivance and competition. At first, as a rule, the men close up their ranks. Her presence creates a complicity amongst them and offers an excellent ground for understanding; the feeling of belonging to the dominant group facing the dominated. Passing remarks about her is, for example, one of the best ways for men to relax and get to know each other. Over a pint, when a woman walks past, or is mentioned, eyes light up and ebbing conversations, lingering over last night's football match, are revived – to not pass comment may even cast a doubt on the silent man's virility. So man delights in appraising the women who walk past, rarely letting slip an opportunity, in speech or writing, to show that, whatever his age, his looks and his occupation, he is also able to appreciate 'the pleasures of life', which are, above all, 'women'. Publicly flaunting his interest in the 'opposite sex' is the usual way for a man to behave; it is a manner of reasserting that not only does he represent humanity in the face of the supposed sub-species constituted by females, but in addition, that he belongs by right to the class which owns all women. And that is precisely where things start going wrong amongst men; for it is rarely a question of common property. The very logic of private property sets them against each other in the battle for the exclusive appropriation of one woman.

The collective appropriation of women does not mean that there is 'joint ownership' of women, where each woman would be considered as common property, to be used indiscriminately by all men: ownership of women is not collectivised. On the contrary, it is interpreted as personal property, which is restricted as far as possible to the titular owner. Certainly, it can sometimes happen that men share the appropriated woman fraternally – in 'gang bangs' for example – but most of the time, each woman gives rise to stiff competition between men, and can lead to grave conflicts of interests sometimes going so far as to break up the best friendships. So that after a while, man becomes tired of going into battle, of having to fight constantly in order to keep up his image and relieve his sexual urges; he decides to bring home a woman and appropriates her for good: he gets married.

7. Marriage

For man, marriage represents a balance between daddy and rapist; legitimate private appropriation, which enables him to take a woman for his varied daily needs. With this acquisition he guarantees himself virtually unlimited use of his wife: she will tirelessly look after his needs, those of his family and his property; she will produce and rear his children, satisfy his sexual drives; sometimes she is even a symbol of his success. By giving his name to a woman he has chosen, and by (more or less) providing her with board and lodging, man offers himself the daily possibility of putting his feet up, putting on shirts which have been washed and ironed, breathing the atmosphere of a well-polished home, watching his offspring grow up, having sex at will, and possibly of showing his wife off in front of his friends. But in seeking to use a woman in this way for his exclusive benefit, he withdraws her from public circulation – she is no longer 'available' for others – and in so doing he creates a situation of conflict within the man class.

The measures men take to restrict tension between themselves and guarantee each one's private property are many and they vary according to different eras and regions. One of the first provisions is usually to codify appropriation by law or by custom; this is usually expressed in a limit on the number of allowed appropriations at the same time by one man. In certain societies it may be possible to have two, three, four wives or more; but Judeo-Christian patriarchy, with the exception of the Mormons, only permits one. Further appropriations are not covered by law and can even lead to judicial proceedings. And so, whereas polygamy held a place of honour among the ancient Hebrews, it is usually punishable by law in modern Western society; similarly the corruption of a minor (a woman who belongs to her father), or borrowing a married woman (a woman who belongs to her husband) are forbidden.

However, legislation pertaining to marriage reflects contra-dictions within the man class and the antagonism between the sexes. The most flagrant paradox is that of the equality between husband and wife proclaimed by ideology and the reality of the appropriation of women sanctioned by law. This ambivalence, which is perpetuated today, appears at the foundation of the Christian church. In 55 DD, Paul, one of the most important early Christian missionaries, taught that 'The wife cannot claim her body as her own; it is her husband's. Equally the husband cannot claim his body as his own; it is his wife's' (I *Corinthians* VII:4). Yet at the same time, he had no qualms about exhorting women to silence and submission: 'Wives, be subject to your husbands; that is your Christian duty' (*Collossians* III:18).

This double-think can be found throughout Christian history, taking different forms in different periods and societies. In France, when the bourgeoisie took over the leadership of (patriarchal) society, they legislated on the appropriation of women according to their own interest – through the civil code of 1804 and the criminal code of 1810 – and they merely added a little bit of 'Liberty, Equality and Fraternity'. To give just one legal example: in the case of borrowing a married woman for sexual purposes, it is not directly a matter of trespassing on the husband's property, but of 'adultery'. The term is sufficiently vague to avoid calling things by their proper name, and makes it possible to put the blame primarily on the appropriated woman (it is therefore up to her to protect herself against intruders). Furthermore, to speak of 'adultery' suggests that there is equality in the appropriation of spouses – man belong-ing to woman as much as woman to man – which is obviously not the case. Until the Criminal Law was modified in 1975, the same word 'adultery' did not have the same significance when applied to the husband as to the wife:

The penalty for adultery deserves comment. Three articles of the Criminal Code (336, 337 and 338) unchanged until 1975, are devoted, in the section 'offences against public morals', to the wife's adultery. The term does not appear in relation to the husband. The definition of the offence is not the same for the two sexes. The wife's adultery consists of a single act, no matter where it is committed; for the husband, only keeping a concubine in the home warrants a sentence (art. 339); to be truthful, it is difficult to imagine such a situation, other than amourous adventures with the servants, the husband then runs little risk.(. . .) The wife can be sent to prison, the husband is liable to pay a mere fine; but, art. 337 generously continues, 'husband retains the power to stop the sentence being put into effect, by consenting to take his wife back' as a result of a veritable right of private pardon. Prison or home: it is up to the husband who demanded the sentence to decide where his wife is to be kept after the judgement. This curious choice makes one think.[1]

Perhaps women have begun to think too much, and perhaps the time has come for the man class to make a few concessions. In any case, since 1975 in France adultery no longer qualifies as an offence, remaining simply grounds for divorce. The law has bowed to the pressure of the 'advanced liberalism' proclaimed by those in government. Subsequently the possibilities of divorce have been extended; the wife is no longer obliged to live with her husband in the place he decides on. Likewise 'the most mediaeval and bloody provision of the French Criminal Code, Art. 324, which authorised the husband to take the law into his own hands and execute his unfaithful wife on the spot, has become a thing of the past.'[2] However, the real impact of these modifications should not be overestimated, for legal provisions are not the only means employed by men to defend their private property, their women. A whole series of measures actually aim to bind the wife to her husband, to confine her to the home, and, occasionally, to render her unattractive or unfit for the sexual use of another man. In addition, to perfect the device granting each man exclusive possession of a woman, the man class endeavours to make it so hard for women outside marriage that women themselves end up wishing to be appropriated.

Women as private property

We have already seen how man manages to get a woman to sacrifice herself in return for his apparent protection and generosity; he generally ensures that his wife is financially dependent on him, and it is not too difficult for him to keep her in the home. His schemes are usually so effective that most of the time he succeeds in persuading her that his own interests are those of the 'couple' or the 'child', and that his advantages are those of his wife. So the famous 'opportunity' she has of staying at home, instead of going to work outside for a boss, is supposed to be one of the great 'privileges' of the married woman.

In actual fact, the only benefit she gets from the situation is to have one boss instead of two; unfortunately, with her husband she has the worst of the two. To give a few examples: domestic labour is not a paid occupation, nor is there any time limit to it (no salary, no 40-hour week, no week-ends, no paid leave, no real retirement); in the case of breach of contract (divorce), her professional experience is considered limited or non-existent – 'Profession? None . . . well, housewife!' – and she will find it all the more difficult to find a paid job, and therefore is all the less likely to want to resign from her 'role' of wife; in a situation of marital tension, if she goes on a cooking, housework or sex strike, the balance of power is obviously very much against her . . . The list of disadvantages of the housewife's condition as compared to that of the wage-earning woman is endless. Yet man can easily tempt his wife to stay at home, as the factory, the supermarket or the typing pool do not exempt her from performing a double day's work. Thus, he can make it seem attractive to not have to go out to work, and to be dependent on only one boss: himself.

The husband does not bind his wife to him through financial blackmail alone; he also tries to confine her as best he can within the home. Although in some countries men traditionally lock their wives up, man does not always need to resort to such measures – especially since men as a whole maintain a rule of terror, in town and countryside, which does not generally encourage women to venture out. So they rarely have to remind their wives of the dangers of going out alone 'for no reason': as a rule, wives restrict these journeys to going between home and work, via the shops and the children's school. If a foolhardy wife ventures out too often, she will be reminded – in the street and at home – that whether she belongs to a man or not, outside the conjugal home, she is 'up for grabs' in just the same way as all other women.

Men as a class put women in such situations that women themselves come to prefer to be married. And it is not only a matter of feeling physically threatened, or of difficulty in finding waged work, but of the existence of a general system aiming to guarantee the exclusive appropriation of at least one woman by each man who so desires.

Ideology and education condemn women to marriage, which is supposed to be the fulfilment of their lives in patriarchy. This is expressed, most sharply, in the many obstacles they have to overcome if they want to fulfil themselves in another way. As far as social success is concerned, it is hardly necessary to underline the fact that a woman has to battle even harder to achieve anything as she constantly has to make people forget which sex she belongs to. It is ludicrous to wish to live one's life through a hierarchy – but access to that hierarchy is still strictly limited according to an anatomical criterion. Besides, it is obvious that the professions and salaries open to men offer far more possibilities to opting out of a regular job and remaining relatively unscathed. To mention one example: skilled manual labour, a field where it is relatively easy to find work, whether temporary, seasonal or off-the-cards (as plumber, electrician, welder, cook, etc.) has very few equivalents for women. Six months' salary for an experienced typist would hardly be sufficient for her to live on for a year; whereas a good season as an assistant chef will sustain a man.

However, money and prestige are not the only things that matter in life, there is also 'love'; and far from being immaterial for a woman, it is considered one of the principal goals of her existence. But, there again, we must not confuse love as applied to men and love as applied to women. Nietzsche, in *The Gay Science*, gives a definition which gives a good glimpse of the ideology of love, and the use that man makes of the emotion:

> The single word love in fact signifies two different things for man and woman. What woman understands by love is clear enough: it is not only devotion, it is a total gift of body and soul, without reservation, without regard for anything whatever. This unconditional nature of her love is what makes it a *faith*, the only one she has. As for man, if he loves a woman, what he *wants* is that love from her; he is in consequence, far from postulating the same sentiment for himself as for woman; if there should be men who also felt that desire for complete abandonment, upon my word, they would not be men.

From the vast collection of stupid remarks about love uttered by men throughout the ages, Simone de Beauvoir picks out one from Balzac: 'At the apex of man's life is fame, at the apex of woman's life is love. Woman is a man's equal only when she makes her life a perpetual offering, as that of man is perpetual action.' And Nietzsche again: 'She demands, therefore, someone to *take* her, someone who does not give himself, who does not abandon himself, but who wishes, on the contrary, to enrich his ego through love . . . The woman gives herself, the man adds to himself by taking her.' In spite of the quantitiy of writings, in poetry, prose and maxims, the general idea is virtually always the same: man in love expects the woman he loves to totally submit to his desires.

Love is, in actual fact, a 'gentle' way of appropriating a woman; it justifies all the restrictions man imposes, and buys all the devotion he demands. And so, in the Christian West, it is one of the pillars – at the same time the method and the justification – of exclusive appropriation, and the man class makes constant ideological use of it. Love stories, for example, whether in literature, pulp-fiction, or the cinema, go straight to the point: when possession is impossible they invariably end with the death of the lovers; otherwise they culminate in the sacrament of marriage. And when the story is over on the screen or on paper, it continues in everyday life, where love becomes a pretext used by man to try and rationalise the free services provided by his wife; it is also a token of his security as proprietor, through the absolute fidelity he requires from his beloved.

The contradictions of appropriation

Man does not always trust love to guarantee the private owner-ship of the vagina and uterus of his wife; he does his best to quell or channel her desires as well, and he often seeks to ren-der her undesirable, or even unfit for sexual use by another man. Practices vary according to place and time, but they have one thing in common: man's preoccupation with being efficient at defending his property, by even the most sordid means

One of man's usual forms of dissuasion is traditionally to institutionalise the wearing of extremely modest clothing by married women (especially when she is outside the home, with-out her husband); a sort of uniform that she must wear to make her less attractive, so that she will not be mistaken for a legally 'available' woman. In some southern European countries, cer-tain wives are only allowed out dressed in black from head to toe. But sometimes men take far more brutal precautions. In feudal times they fastened heavy chastity belts round their wives before leaving for crusades, and these belts have attracted quite a following; even today, a British inventor who has per-fected lighter model claims to be doing excellent business. Then again, in several African countries – including Somalia, Sudan and Ethiopia – for centuries, men have not been content with the customary infibulation of their daughters, they also sew-up their wives in the case of a long absence, for example, or if they do not want them for intercourse.

These two types of torture which are either a thing of the past or are only practised in certain cultures, are connected with repressing sexuality in women, and this is universal throughout history and the world. This repression aims to systematically stifle, from childhood, women's sexual desires. Methods vary from one place to another: it can be a matter purely and simply of removing the tip or ablating the entire clitoris, likewise of eliminating all the external genital organs apart from the labia majora (in 1979 in Africa the estimated number of women and young girls mutilated in this way was 74 million).[3] Sexual repression can also take on a more 'civilised' form; Judeo-Christian patriarchy has been very successful so far, notably through science and the church, in constantly repressing women's sexuality.

Yet such measures present two major disadvantages for the husband. On the one hand, whatever the methods used, their effectiveness is invariably limited by man's very notion of sexuality (nothing will stop him in his desire to appropriate, and, on the contrary, the more inaccessible a woman is, the greater the challenge to possess her); on the other hand, by protecting his property in this way, the husband restricts his own sexual use of his wife. As a consequence of doing his utmost to repress her desires, he ends up having problems in using her or appreciating her himself. He frequently complains, like this *Playboy* reader who is asking for a solution to the problem that he brought on himself:

> I have been married for nearly fifteen years. About three times a week I have the impression I am raping my wife. Rape? In any case, that's the term Germaine Greer would use if she knew me. But what else can I do? My wife does not want a divorce. It is out of the question, because of the children, her parents, etc. I don't want to be unfaithful to her. I have neither the time nor the inclination to chase women, and I must admit, I still love my wife. And so when I 'demand' it, she 'gives in', waits patiently until I've finished with her eyes glued to the ceiling. This hurts me a lot, it even affected my performance for a while and then I made the best of it. Has Germaine Greer a solution, she who claims to know all the answers?[4]

When his wife does not want to make love, and he is no longer satisfied with repeatedly raping her, the husband always has prostitutes to turn to, or adultery, which is, for man, an extension of marriage. That is why, in the nineteenth century and at the beginning of the twentieth, during the 'belle epoque' of the triumphant bourgeoisie, brothels were all the rage and the fashionable bourgeois had both a wife and a mistress. There were a whole variety of courtesans, demi-mondaines and whores; and the husband could appropriate the woman he wanted completely legally, as long as he did not constantly do it in his own home, or in the home of the woman's owner (if he did, it was at his own risk). Moral order under the bourgeoisie easily collapsed into unholy disorder which, in time, would have been a serious threat to the institution of marriage. And so, the specialists, who are taking things in hand more and more, try today to put things right and restore order in the home.

We have already seen some of the legal modifications made in France in order to bring the law in line with the new ideology, but the overall project is in fact much more ambitious than it first appears: it is an attempt to transcend the eternal contradiction of private appropriation by at last providing the husband with a woman who will be simultaneously a wife and a mistress. The offensive is led (in particular) by the sexologists who do their best to make marriage sound more attractive by adding, as a bonus, the hope of multiple orgasms for the woman. In short, they have brought 'sex' out of the catacombs of Christianity, to usher it into the new household of the deserving executive; and publications aimed at women rapidly followed suit. From the beginning of the seventies, each magazine began to hum the same tune, through adverts as much as the articles. *Amour* of April 1974 suggests, backed up by examples: 'And if he were to be unfaithful to me with another me . . .' *Lou*, at the same time, was selling its bra 'Certitude' using the same ideology: 'It is not because you are a mother that men will no longer look at you as a woman.' *Marie-Claire* of February 1973 was even more specific, and evaluated women's going rate on the market: 'The wife is the new star. Mistresses are going down, lawful wives are going up. She now holds all the trumps to become that rare bird; the married mistress. It only takes the guts . . .' The accompanying photo showed a woman, evoking Marilyn Monroe, lasciviously sprawled across a washing machine, with Place Clichy, a red light-district, in the background.

The idea has been so successful that it is sometimes hard to imagine that, only ten or fifteen years ago, the married woman's image was totally different. The woman who enjoys sex no longer risks being burnt at the stake, and being automatically considered hysterical: on the contrary, she will be praised by *Cosmopolitan*. At the same time, the husband finds it difficult to honour all the clauses in the new property contract proposed to him.

In their effort to do away with one of the contradictions in marriage, the specialists have, in fact, created another: the husband now finds himself responsible for providing not only board and lodging but also for his wife's 'right to pleasure'. It is more than he bargained for; in most cases he would have been happy to be able to continue coming in peace, rather than have to worry about giving his wife an orgasm. If she insists on strict adherence to the new convention, it only needs him to fail to satisfy her demands for there to develop a ground for conflict. It is obvious that this change in conjugal sex is not always appreciated by the man class. But is this new source of irritation not a necessary evil for the husband: could the competent authorities have left matters as they were?

The balance of power within marriage has changed considerably, in Judeo-Christian patriarchy, since the beginning of the century; reflecting contradictions between patriarchal organisation and the capitalist mode of production. The power conferred by law on the husband, for example, has been seriously whittled down from the point of view of the wife's financial dependence. In France, until 1907, civil law did not allow a married woman to work outside the home without her husband's permission, nor to receive her own salary herself. The law of 13 July 1907 enabled her to dispose of her salary; with the law of 18 February 1938 she no longer had to obtain permission to work outside the home (although the husband maintained the right to oppose it), and finally, the law of 13 July 1965 granted her the 'right to follow a profession without the husband's consent' (art. 273). The married woman has obtained, over the years, the legal basis for (potential) financial independence; not necessarily as a result of any benevolent feelings on the part of the man class, but simply because it is in the logic of the economy itself. Moreover, this antagonism between patriarchal and capitalist interests does not look as if it is likely to be reduced:

> The appearance of products manufactured with a higher efficiency in the commodity economy, which are increasingly replacing domestic products, will draw a growing proportion of women into wage-earning activities. This trend does not seem easily reversable.[5]

The number of married women working for a wage outside the home has increased in most western countries. This situation implies not only limitation on the husband's power to blackmail, but it also presents an explosive contradiction: the wife's simultaneous position as wage-earner outside the home where she sells her labour power, and husband's property in the home where she is used endlessly. This opposition which has been clearly highlighted by Colette Guillaumin,[6] can only exacerbate the man–woman conflict within the conjugal unit, and the husband's authority is likely to continue to ebb.

In addition to the various legal alterations to the marriage contract over the last hundred years, in most countries in the West new laws have been passed which have fundamentally changed relations between the sex classes. These are the laws authorising women to use a means of contraception, followed by the legalisation of abortion (1969 in the UK, 1975 in France) as a result of campaigns by the feminist movement. Thus, in the space of a few years, the man class has well and truly lost a major part of its power over women – the unrestricted appropriation of their wombs.

It is certain that such a historical landmark is an important contribution towards the struggle for the destruction of patriarchy. Although often imperceptible on a macro-social level, it is nevertheless the case that feminist ideas are seeping into every household, disturbing the relations between the sexes. This, together with the various contradictions already mentioned, make it highly probable that man will find it increasingly difficult, inside as well as outside marriage, to defend and realise his ownership rights over women.

To package the measures that aim to guarantee him the exclusive appropriation of a woman, man traditionally presents marriage as his sacrifice; the renunciation of his life as a bachelor, and the end of his freedom, which he offers as a token of 'love' to the woman he marries. In so doing, he joins the ranks of all the masters in history who invariably guaranteed the real sacrifice of their slaves through what appeared to be their own sacrifice. But at the same time he is unaware that his condition of proprietor, which enables him to satisfy a certain number of needs, provides him with only very mediocre pleasures. In fact, men have always complained about the paltriness of their relations with women – look at the floods of tears shed in songs, poetry and pubs about Impossible Love which dies in marriage or is fulfilled in death – they have wept a great deal without ever realising that they were responsible for their own misfortune. There is actually no love which is possible in a relationship of appropriation, and there can be no question of a human relationship between two people when one of them is considered as an object. A man gets impoverished pleasure from possessing a woman, a pleasure which bears no comparison to that which two free individuals could experience together.

8. Between men

Relations between men centre around the struggle for power; whether individually or in a group, they are permanent rivals in the appropriation of women, wealth and glory. Friendship itself, so often proclaimed a typically masculine sentiment, is more a pact of non-aggression, a brief respite from the fight, than a genuine pleasure in being together: it is no more than a delicate balance between competition and being on the watch. The slightest incident is enough to tip the scales. At the tiniest hope of victory, the fragile truce is, as often as not, cheerfully broken.

It does not generally occur to man that he can establish non-competitive relationships; he constantly needs to measure himself and place himself on a hierarchical ladder. Hierarchy is not only his principle of organisation within patriarchy, but simultaneously the means and the end of his struggle for power – it is the framework for his relations and the ground on which he fulfils himself. And so he gets involved in endless conflicts in order to climb the rungs, which he experiences on an individual level by a great variety of blows and knocks, and, socially, by total shambles – war, crisis, famine, pollution, plunder, murder, robbery. And yet, in spite of the damage caused by these battles, he still considers hierarchy necessary, and he usually sees its absence – anarchy – as a synonym for chaos.

The key relationship between men, the one that shapes and symbolises all the others, is the father–son relationship: it is both the crucible in which the hierarchical relationship is forged, and the characteristic form adopted by relationships between men. From birth, the son sees the father as the representative of power, he who, among the human beings around him, commands authority – 'Daddy knows everything, daddy's the strongest.' He looks at him, eyes wide with admiration; then his expression clouds over with apprehension as he waits for approbation or reproof.

Faced with the weakness and obvious ignorance of the child, the father does not give information, nor does he formulate an opinion: he decrees and enforces a sentence; he uses his strength and his knowledge as the instruments and justification of his power. He sees in his son the mirror of his own dependence and he wants to make him into an image of his success: through his son he can avenge his own childhood and make him the counterbalance to the share of humiliation he endures every day. He does not let the child construct his own life; on the contrary, he projects the fulfilment of a good many of his fantasies on to him. In one way or another, he soon begins to teach him to become a 'man': that is to submit to power so that he in turn will be able to exercise it. The father thus instils in his son a pattern of behaviour that the son will encounter and reproduce in his relations with men, and in which, no matter how high you get, there is always someone higher.

From an early age, the son does not judge his actions by his own experiences and perception of the world, but admires and despises himself through the eyes of his father. His discoveries, his creations and his games are lost in his anxiety about his father's judgement – what must he do to be like Daddy, to please Daddy, annoy Daddy, beat Daddy. Of course, at school, the image of the infallible father fades, but the pattern has been set, and the ground lost by one father is gained by another: a teacher, a coach, a stronger and more experienced friend . . . the dance of the fathers has begun. And it will continue through the various stages of the child's formation (family, school and factory, high school and university, army) and accompany the son with a changing rhythm, an unchanging tune: 'You don't know anything. Daddy knows everything.' Whether from the mouth of the sergeant of the marine corps – 'You're an arsehole': 'Yes Sergeant!' – or from the distinguished lips of a university professor, the message rarely varies: you must learn to obey to be able to give orders, and to think like daddy to be authoritative.

Throughout his education, the boy revolves round his father; both the judge of his success and reference point, his father is the symbol of success and he who ratifies it. He designates the most deserving son, distributes rewards and punishments, decorations or solitary confinement, as he sees fit; he is the judge of good behaviour. But, his position is coveted, and in time, the son will start competing with him.

The son is brought up according to the principle 'be a slave and you will become master', but he is so used to obeying and submitting that he will invariably seek shelter under the protection of authority to justify his thoughts and acts. The marks of his initiation are so deeply engraved in him that his eventual rebellion against his father is usually not more than the substitution of another one: he rids himself of one judge to create another of his choice. And so he goes through libraries looking for intellectual guides who will think for him, or he becomes a member of a party that will analyse for him, or he relies on a leader of a gang or organisation: in any case, whatever his tastes may be, his only difficulty is in selection, for fathers are like weeds – they grow everywhere.

And when he feels he can at last become a father himself, that little by little he can take possession of the scraps of power that are his due, he does not necessarily escape the logic of initiation. From the height of his rostrum, from the depths of his armchair or ensconced behind his presidential desk, he remains the child spellbound by daddy, the pupil, fascinated by the master – the son who, in short, is nothing without the father. The situation is absurd but the chain is endless: the father represents authority and hands it on to the son, while he himself is no more than a son under a father's authority. This ridiculous state of affairs is aptly illustrated by the famous mystery of the Christian God, where man reproduces himself by being the Father and the Son united by Holy Virility.

Hierarchy: man's prison

Man never becomes the Father he likes to imagine; he flounders between submission and domination. At no point is he in control of his own life; he manages only to accumulate more or less power over the lives of others. Virility, which is the spirit governing his entire existence, is a permanent struggle to assert his power and it drives him to engage in a perpetual battle, which is expressed in a series of victories and defeats. And so, being a 'man' is not only winning and believing oneself to be the strongest, it is also knowing how to lose and bow to a stronger force; knowing how to fit in between orders given and orders taken.

'There's a time to bite and a time to lick boots.' Man often likes to compare himself with a dog, and after obediently giving his master his paw, he generally has no qualms about barking and showing his teeth. Is not one of the most prized examples of virility the sergeant major, nicely wedged between his superiors and his men? And even when he climbs the rungs, man does not escape the logic of hierarchy, for hierarchy is without end. There is never a human being at the top, 'supreme power' is never concentrated in one man, it is only delegated to representatives. All the masters of history, even the most powerful, have always paid for their power with submission of some kind; thus, the feudal lords, who crushed their vassals and sapped the lives of their serfs, had to bow to the authority of their king, who, in turn, through the church, was subject to his god, who ultimately only existed nailed to a cross.

All leaders must inevitably respect oaths of allegiance and make various sacrifices; besides, they only hold what is a small fragment of power. All men endeavour to increase their own portion, they are engaged in endless fights, and the strongest even try to eliminate each other, in the vain hope that they will no longer have to share their power. During these combats, all is fair – from political murder to world war – and in their quest for total power, the leaders are never guarded against their own weaknesses, against a military defeat or against the assassination which awaits them.

The power of the 'greatest' has always been precarious; they tried to establish their power in blood but often came to a quick and wretched end. And so Alexander died of malaria in Babylon when he was barely 33, Napoleon perished alone in the

South Atlantic like an abandoned dog, and Caesar, who thought hierarchy had nothing to offer unless viewed from above – 'I'd rather be first in this village than second in Rome' – was stabbed 23 times. As for the new masters, their power is no more assured than was that of their predecessors: it always hangs by a thread. When they are not dependent on the constant jiggery-pokery and the hazard of purges inside a central committee, they unfailingly lay themselves open to the inefficiency of their bodyguards, the clumsiness of their television make-up or the consequences of a badly orchestrated campaign.

Whatever the dangers and difficulties he has to face, man generally sets his heart on becoming boss at any price: the pettiness of the great rarely puts him off, and as a rule he will stop at nothing to increase his share of power. Through the ages, his thirst for power has been the source of a long river of blood, which, thanks to the enormous technological developments of the last few years, flows at an increasingly rapid rate (first world war: about 9 million dead; second world war: more than 40 million dead). But modern heroes know how to do things in style, and on the day of victory, as often as not, they shroud themselves in the mantle of civilisation; Eisenhower, for example, on being granted the freedom of the City of London in July 1945, declared with style: 'Modesty must be the natural reaction of the man who receives acclaim that cost him the blood of his subordinates and the sacrifice of his friends.' Which still did not stop him from parading in his general's uniform – modesty had doubtless effaced the blood stains. Today's generation of leaders – who can, at will, blow up the planet – has lost in lyricism what it has gained in candour. Henry Kissinger, who was personally responsible for some of the bombings of North Vietnam, stated plainly and complacently what is behind the perpetual struggle between men: 'Power is the ultimate aphrodisiac.'

Man invariably seeks his pleasure between the bars of the hierarchy principle. He locks up his own life in it and makes the world little short of unbearable, but, in most cases, he has no doubts: it does not occur to him that fulfilment is possible outside the struggle for power. This obsession is not restricted to a

chosen powerful few. It can be found at the bottom of the hierarchical ladder as well as at the top, and is expressed by the loss
of the self in identification with the leader who himself identifies
with either the cause, the people, the nation, or, more
modestly, with the party, the team or the common good. The
mechanism works quite simply: the leader thrives on the life
and blood of his men, who in return receive crumbs of his
power and glory; obviously, these diminish as the pyramid gets
wider, but, nevertheless, at all levels, each one gets his share.
Napoleon, who in his time could boast of some authentic mas-
sacres, is a good illustration of this process. The day after the
Battle of Rivoli, he addressed a good number of future corpses
thus:

> Soldiers, you rushed like a torrent from the heights of the
> Appenines . . . You won battles without cannons, crossed
> rivers without bridges, went on forced marches without
> boots, bivouacked without brandy and often without
> bread . . . And when, after a glorious victory, you return
> home, your fellow-citizens will point you out saying: 'They
> were of the Italian campaign.'

A man's problem is to choose the right cause and put himself
in the hands of the right leader; then all he has to do is to throw
himself headlong into the fray, until he ends up either dead or
covered in glory. But he must be prudent and perceptive, for an
error of judgement can be costly: apart from the notoriety and
the defeat, it can lead the survivor into the war criminal's dock
or a forced labour camp. But man generally jibs at nothing in
the hope of reaping the laurels of victory: he sets off in 1914 for
Berlin, flower in his gun and smile on his lips, and even if he
comes back in 1918 with his face smashed up in battle, he has
fine tales to tell and lovely war memorials to adorn. This race
for power and glory in which very few refuse to participate, is
exacerbated in an obvious way in military activities. When the
existing hierarchies are out of reach, man undertakes to create
a new one – within a local gang, a left-wing organisation, or
some 'alternative' project.

Relations between men in patriarchy are based on the fundamental principle of integration into and identification with a hierarchy. It is a principle whose basic corollary is that each fragment of power acquired – whether it be the general or sergeant-major, chief of police or gang leader, little boss or big boss, head of anybody or anything whatsoever, and even as a last resort, head of the household – enables man to offer himself identification at less personal cost through a substitute: the son.

Victory has its joys, but fighting has its dangers, so, as soon as he has the opportunity, man sends somebody else to fetch the laurels that he would like to wear himself. Indeed, in the logic of identification with a hierarchy, it is of little importance whether or not he actually takes part in the combat, provided that, when the battle is over, the spectator can identify with their triumph. A good example of this process is the football supporter who, at the end of the match, chants 'we won' or cries 'we lost'. This is a feature of all organised competitive relations: rather than give of himself man generally seeks through the acquisition of a fragment of power – a place on the terraces can be quite sufficient – to leave it up to the others to build up the image of his glory and the arms of his might. This general attitude, reproduced at all levels and in different forms, always hinges on the same basic principle: the father instils all the powers of virility in the son so that the father will then go out and get himself killed in his father's name and stead. That is how man creates stadium heroes who all go out on the pitch for the prestige of the nation, work heroes who sweat their guts out for the good of the party, and children who are massacred for the honour of their fathers.

As man climbs up the hierarchical ladder, his share of the glory increases, and the risks to which he exposes himself diminish; yet, even when he is almost at the summit, and his influence appears greatest, his power is never total and the risks he runs are never eliminated. He remains in permanent conflict as he tries to defend and increase his share of power. Look at the antics of today's statesmen in their attempts to ensure their re-election; on the other hand, all the 'great men' who clutter up history only truly become so after their deaths. We have seen, for example, how Alexander, Caesar and Napoleon came to rather ridiculous ends; as for the great men whose hours of glory are still fresh in our minds – Hitler, Stalin and Mao, to name but three – their power obviously rested on such a fragile base, that they had to reinforce it with secret police and ideological terror. Those who were not defeated by their rivals, fell from grace a very short time after being buried.

History: a power struggle between men

The history of patriarchy is the history of the appropriation of women and of the struggle for power among men: the story, in short, of the division of human beings into masters and slaves, and the resulting antagonism. Since the beginning of patriarchal organisation, the condition of women has been quite simple. Appropriated, they are always automatically slaves. The condition of men, on the other hand, is more complex and historically less stable. In fact, the victories or the defeats they encounter in the permanent conflict they are engaged in are expressed and socially embedded in relations of greater or lesser appropriation. Some men have often been purely and simply excluded by the winners of their sex class – have no longer been acknowledged as 'men' – as a result of their own defeat, or the institutionalisation of the defeat of their fathers. And so, in patriarchy, men can also be slaves, and are engaged in two types of struggle: on the one hand that of the masters – mainly through wars of hegemony, political combat and economic rivalry – and, on the other, the struggle of the slaves against the power of their masters.

The struggles men are engaged in have developed in patriarchal societies with different modes of production – slave labour, feudal or capitalist, for instance – but such that, until recently, the dominant minority lived in opulence resulting from the labour and wretchedness of the majority. Power was therefore directly linked to an obvious material interest, and the slaves rebelled both against being excluded from power, and against the material conditions in which they had to somehow survive.

In other words, the struggles between masters and slaves depend not only on a conflict within the man class, but also on the 'contradition between the productive forces and the relations of productions' (Marx, *Communist Manifesto*). This double mainspring of historical evolution can be found in all the great revolts of the past; however, the male slaves rose up first and foremost to conquer, or re-conquer the position they felt was their due inside their sex class. The most common war cry the male insurgents would yell in the faces of their masters has been: 'We are not slaves, we too are men!' Weapons in hand, they have often tried to retrieve the share of power they considered 'naturally' belonged to them, since they were 'men' in a patriarchal society. At the instigation of Spartacus – a former shepherd from Thrace reduced to slavery – thousands of slaves sought to escape from the Roman Empire to regain possession of their rights, their women and their country. One of the first peasant revolts in France (in 1067) was that of the serfs of Viry, who rose up against the provost and canons of Notre Dame in Paris, in whose power was their right to marry. The serfs wanted to dispense with their requiring the monks' permission to appropriate, through marriage, the woman of their choice.

In keeping with the conflicts between them and the development of the productive forces, large numbers of men have, throughout history, been reduced to slavery, and as the genitals are the basic criteria for the division into masters and slaves in patriarchy, so castration has frequently been the result of the exclusion of one group of men from the power race. It was common practice in ancient times, and even if today it is definitely less widespread, some still feel their oppression as 'castration', that is, as the destruction of the patriarchal symbol of their power. Raoul Vaneigem puts as follows the idea doubtless present in many men's minds: 'Regimes agreeably baptised "democratic" merely humanise castration.'[1] This situation – whatever form the exclusion from the sharing in the division of power takes – obviously engenders permanent antagonism inside the man class, which historically fairly stable in its social manifestation, took, from the nineteenth century onwards, a new direction in Judeo-Christian patriarchy.

Indeed, that is when men seriously began to conceive the project of a 'whole man' who would develop outside the hierarchy and the struggle for power. Yet, in spite of being a step in the right direction, this 'whole man' did not really represent humankind, but clearly implied only the male of the species. Between 1918 and 1921, in the anarchist Ukraine, one of the greatest victories of the anti-hierarchical struggle inside the man class took place. Nestor Makhno – who was nicknamed 'Batko', that is, 'Father' – made some elegant speeches during the insurrection:

> Win or die – that is the dilemma facing the peasants and workers of the Ukraine at this historic moment. But we cannot all die, we are innumerable. We are Humanity! And so, we shall win . . . We shall not win only to repeat the errors of the past: to place our fate in the hands of new masters. We shall win in order to take our destiny into our own hands, to organise our lives according to our own will and with our truth.[2]

But when Makhno (rightly) spoke of the emancipation of humanity, that did not prevent him, in his everyday behaviour, from restricting membership of humankind. Voline, who took part in Makhno's insurrectionary campaign, writes: 'The second shortcoming of Makhno and many of his close associates – commanders and others – was their attitude towards women. Especially when inebriated, these men indulged in inadmissible acts – hateful would be more exact – going so far as to force certain women to participate in orgies.'[3] Women then were so little a part of the 'humanity' of the Ukraine libertarians that Voline considered raping them as a mere 'shortcoming', and a secondary one at that, less serious than Makhno's 'great fault' which he considered to be 'alcohol abuse'.

During the Civil War, Spanish women also found there were limitations to men's success in the fight against hierarchy. The anarchist, Lucia Sanchez Saornil saw, for example: 'a number of homes, not only those of CNT members but true anarchists (!?) ruled according to the purest feudal principles',[4] and she had to persist in trying to make her 'comrades' notably in the FAI and the CNT, understand that 'woman . . . also belongs to the human species'. She confronted one of them with the following evidence:

> You, can you imagine a bourgeois saying that the workers should be emancipated? So, if you find it logical that, like the bourgeois with the worker, the anarchist as a man keeps woman chained up, *it is absurd to hear him shout 'women must be emancipated'*. And if he does shout it, how can one not say to him 'you start'.[5]

During the struggles they have waged against the power of their masters, male slaves have rarely questioned their own status as masters in the relations between the sex classes. Men who call themselves revolutionaries have, in most cases, perpetuated in their behaviour and their writings, the appropriation of women. Besides, some still like to forge concepts such as 'main front' and 'secondary front', while their wives cook, wash up and guarantee them a hero's welcome. As for the fate reserved for the women – wives and daughters – of the defeated rulers, it is generally hardly any different from that of their other material possessions: if they are unfortunate enough not to have been able to escape, in most cases they are raped while the house is plundered. Eldridge Cleaver went so far as to describe rape as an 'insurrectionary act'.[6] On the whole, men have tried to make the revolution a matter between themselves, in which women stayed in the position they were traditionally granted inside patriarchal organisation. Thus they attempted to restrict women's participation in the struggle, and subsequently did their best to keep quiet about the part women nevertheless played by sanctifying sometimes one – Red or Black Virgin – to conceal, behind her glorious image, the reality of the battle of all the others. During the Paris Commune, for instance, women played a fundamental role from the beginning of the uprising, because of their very condition of appropriation. Indeed, on 18 March 1871, when General Lecomte and his men had already begun to bring down the famous cannons from the Butte, the women of Montmartre quickly thronged the streets for, as always, they had risen very early to fetch the milk. They were then joined by the men whom they had roused, but women were still, according to all accounts, more numerous in the crowd. And the events which followed give a fairly good idea of the fragility of power when men at last cease to defend it. Henri Lefebvre plausibly describes what happened:

> The dense crowd surrounds the soldiers and paralyses the transportation of the cannons. Knots of people form. They club together to offer food and wine to the hungry and thirsty men (they had not brought their kit bags). They chat. They shout: 'Long live the army!' The bars and cabarets are opened. Housewives go back up to fetch their modest supplies and spread them on the tables for the soldiers. The crowd fêtes and regales them. Some soldiers even exchange their guns for a glass of wine. The effervescent mass becomes a community, becomes communion.
>
> The women openly criticise the officers; they address them without worrying about hierarchy and without a trace of military respect: 'Where are you taking these cannons? To Berlin?' The ranks broke, closed up again, broke again, under the cries and threats of the officers.
>
> General Lecomte realises too late the danger the throng presents for his troops, submerging them, throwing them back into everyday life. He has forgotten, if ever he knew it, one of the tactical principles of civil war: never let soldiers come into contact with civilians. He gives the order to fire if the crowd approaches to within thirty steps around 8.30 a.m. and he is not obeyed.[7]

From mutiny to barricades, the town rose up. During the whole of that day, there was only one real fight, at Place Pigalle, lasting barely twenty minutes. Paris woke up the following morning without a state. There was neither army nor police force, for those who remained had fled to Versailles under cover of darkness. On that day, did women still have to rise early to fetch the milk? History is silent about that. But it does tell us how men immediately began to reconstruct power through a central committee, and how it was subsequently re-established as a republic after a bloodbath in which 30,000 men and women were shot on the orders of butcher Adolphe Thiers.

Up till now, men have always guarded power well, either as they benefited by submitting to it, or as they have reproduced it by fighting it. All the rebellions and revolutions in the past were defeated by their own limitations. All they did was offer an increasingly brighter glimmer of hope for our future. Those which were supposedly victorious did not signify much more than a change of masters. However, if the taking over of the economy by the bourgeoisie and its political consequences did not really alter, the hierarchical organisation of men and the appropriation of women in Judeo-Christian patriarchy, it did radically change their dynamics.

Whereas all the confrontations between masters and slaves in the past had ended in the defeat of the latter, and the upholding of the existing production relations, the final victory of the bourgeoisie over the feudal power system meant, on the contrary, the break-up of previous relations of production. By making the development of the productive forces the vehicle of their power, the bourgeoisie gave historical evolution, until then bogged down in relative stability, a dynamic form. Marx describes this change in perspective:

> Constant revolutionising of production, uninterrupted
> disturbance of all social conditions, everlasting
> uncertainty and agitation distinguish the bourgeois epoch
> from all earlier ones. All fixed, frozen relations, with their
> train of ancient and venerable prejudices and opinions,
> are swept away, all new-formed ones become antiquated
> before they can ossify. All that is solid melts into air, all
> that is holy is profaned, and man is at last compelled to
> face, with sober senses, his real conditions of life, and his
> relations with his kind.[8]

The very logic of bourgeois power, then that of the bureaucrats and specialists who followed, has, in fact, created the material conditions for human emancipation. Not exactly for the reasons Marx believed, but because the development of the productive forces within patriarchy had brought to a head not only the contradictions in the struggle for power, but also the antagonism between the sex classes.

By making the development and organisation of the economy the instrument of their power, the bourgeoisie, bureaucrats and experts have created, in Judeo-Christian patriarchy, such abundance, that the struggle for power between men no longer even has the pretext of material gain. Whereas the power of the feudal lords directly procured the well-being that their domination over the majority guaranteed them, and that of the nineteenth-century bourgeoisie was a direct consequence of the wealth they derived from the exploitation of the majority, the power of the bureaucrats and experts depends today only on their apparent ability to guarantee the well-being of the majority they organise. In patriarchal societies with a capitalist mode of production – private or state – it is no longer a matter of money bringing power, but of power possibly bringing money. The power of present leaders is only accompanied incidentally by material advantages which, are generally much the same as those enjoyed by most members of the man class. Thus the French President drives at 80 mph down the same motorway and in the same Peugeot 504 as any travelling salesman, and he even has to have cosmetic changes made to his Boeing jet if he is not to travel in exactly the same conditions as a charter passenger. Power is now so far removed from real material gain that some of the most powerful trade union leaders in France and other countries have salaries similar to that of a skilled labourer.

Power rid of its eternal alibi appears today as an end in itself, the necessary and sufficient condition for its existence. Hierarchy, which in patriarchy had nearly always been presented as the only viable form of social organisation, is revealed for what it always has been: the means and the end of the struggle between men for power.

By developing the productive forces and smashing the ancient feudal hierarchy based on divine support, the bourgeoisie have crushed the material and religious justifications for hierarchical organisation. They have broadened the competitive field to such an extent within the man class that, at present, in developed industrial patriarchy, most men can 'fulfil' themselves through the hierarchical divisions but at the same time fulfilment through hierarchy has never looked so derisory as it does today. The new representatives of power are but a pale caricature of the ancient masters, their power and their lives have shrunk away. While the feudal lords went happily to war, never deigning to work, and the nineteenth-century bourgeoisie stuffed themselves while they watched their capital grow, today's specialists and bureaucrats hang on to their fragment of power, working themselves to death in trying to manage the unmanageable. And, if the few who are at the heads of the most powerful states dispose of a potential power that the rulers of the past did not have, unfortunately for them they cannot use it without blowing up a large part of the planet.

It is no longer out of the question to ask who could really want this power, whose most illustrious representatives, with their zombie-like faces, are reminiscent of the gladiators of old who were given to the public for the circus games. The absurdity of the rat race is not only apparent at the top of the ladder, it is also illustrated by the favourite son of developed industrial patriarchy: the executive. Second fiddle to the specialist whose science he imbibes and from whom he gathers crumbs of power, he is the latest symbol of virile glory: the new model in which man seeks fulfilment.

The executive easily adapts the ideas from his brief period of student revolt in the sixties to fit his life in the eighties. After eight hours of work, five days a week, 48 weeks a year, 40 years a lifetime, adventure for him is still just around the corner from his office. For he is not bourgeois since he is always ready to jump on the bandwagon of fashion and he surrounds himself with amusing little gadgets or brings up his children 'progressively' not forgetting, when necessary, to accept the responsibility for that important component of 'the quality of life' which is his 'meaningful relationship' (recently he has even grasped that the dishwasher had to be loaded and unloaded . . .). The executive is constantly in search of new sensations – he believes in the advertising slogan that the 'world is his oyster'. Not for him the consumerism of the masses – he has select guide books to tell him what to read, to eat and what amplifier to buy. And when he goes to Corsica or Jamaica it is not a vulgar package holiday but it is somewhere different and 'unknown' which only he (and the million other readers of *The Sunday Times*) is aware of.

Today the economy produces illusions for which material goods are merely a backcloth – the lost potential of a sports car stuck in an eight-mile traffic jam; the illusion of happiness on an overcrowded beach, between a polluted sea and built-up dunes; a gastronomical 'celebration' with frozen prawns, flavourless pâté, battery-fed chicken, wine that has been tampered with, etc. The illusion of life, of pleasure, of power – for in developed industrial patriarchy, man can nearly always 'fulfil' himself inside one of the numerous available hierarchies. In any case, consumption offers him such a vast and varied field of action in which to 'express' himself and compete, that he can, as a last resort, have access to it by theft.

Self-realisation through the possession of power symbols has become so democratic, for Western man, that the trappings of power are becoming meaningless: almost every man has a car, but nobody can move; more and more take their families on holiday, but it is only to crowd together further and further away; many can afford fresh trout but the trout no longer have any taste. Hierarchy is bordering on the absurd, to the point where if, for instance, each Frenchman realised his supposed 'dream' – a house with a garden – there would not even be enough room for the cows to graze.

Today, patriarchy is at the end of its history; in its most deve-loped form, it has created many ways of freeing people from natural alienation, whilst at the same time reproducing, to a degree of extreme sophistication, the most inhuman law of nature: that of the survival of the fittest. The struggle for power between men has made the world unfit to live in; where people do not die of hunger, life is reduced to waiting for death, day by day, amidst an accumulation of commodities and pollution. Judeo-Christian patriarchy has developed the productive forces until they have invaded every facet of life and every place on earth – even giving itself the power to destroy the planet. At present, patriarchy has almost reached the limits of material expansion and the economy is inevitably plunging into a crisis; whilst among the thousands of lethal missiles dispersed all over the globe, some are beginning to go rusty in their silos. It is becoming increasingly difficult to prevent a nuclear holocaust, and we have to walk around with blinkers on not to 'have in front of us at every moment the empirical confirmation of the Marxian theory of accumulation, the crisis of capital'.[9] The race for power is obviously about to end in disaster and everybody is so aware of this that nobody wants to believe it.

In their rise to power the bourgeoisie have done away with the religious foundation for the hierarchisation of human beings. In doing this, they have set in motion a process leading to the dissolution of the most basic hierarchy, that between men and women. The Women's struggle, which has become more vigorous since the end of the sixties, is the struggle of history's first and last slaves. Likewise the last obstacle in the way of human emancipation seems today to be the first master: man. Representative of power and its most ardent defender – intellectual, politician, policeman, soldier, magistrate, daddy, rapist and boss in every shape and size – man reproduces all the patriarchal values, to the point of embodying the very power that oppresses him: he is in the ridiculous position of being both guarantor and victim of the system.

And so, when a man is suffocated by the paltriness of his existence, and he tries to put an end to power once and for all, he need not go far to find the enemy: his struggle is first and foremost within himself. Getting rid of the 'man' buried inside him is the first step for a man aiming to rid himself of power. The death warrant of patriarchy will come about either in nuclear self-destruction (will it then be able to rise from its ashes?) or in the actions of free and autonomous individuals, united in their comon desire to live without power. Up to now the flames of hope never burned for long, but a few weeks in May 1968 showed once more, through the wave of occupations in France, what path the elimination of the state and the realisation of generalised self-management could take. In its final defeat, the nineteenth-century proletariat bequeathed us its greatest victory: the discovery of the potential organisation of society into a federation of councils. Today we know how to achieve emancipation. The pleasure of living without power may give the push that will finally tip the scales of history.

Notes

1. Introduction

1. Margaret Mead: *Sex and Temperament in Three Primitive Societies*, London, Routledge, 1935.
2. Robert Briffault: *The Mothers*, London, Macmillan, 1927.
3. Pierre Samuel: *Amazones, Guerrières et Gaillardes*, Brussels, Editions Complexe, 1975.
4. Robert Stoller: *Sex and Gender*, London, Hogarth, 1968.
5. Raoul Vaneigem: *Traité de Savoir-Vivre à l'Usage des Jeunes Générations*, Paris, Gallimard, 1967.
6. François Jacob: 'Sexualité et Diversité Humaine', *Le Monde*, 9, 10, 11 and 12 February 1979.
7. Simone de Beauvoir: *The Second Sex*, Harmondsworth, Penguin, 1972.
8. Monique Wittig: *Questions Féministes*, no. 8, May 1980.
9. Christine Delphy: *Questions Féministes*, no. 7, February 1980.
10. J. Bachofen: *Myth, Religion and Mother-Right*, London, Routledge & Kegan Paul, 1967.
11. Ernest Borneman: *Das Patriarchat*, Frankfurt, S. Fisher Verlag, 1975.
12. Raoul Vaneigem: *Traité de Savoir-Vivre*.

2. Man and his body

1. Joseph Dietzgen: *The Nature of Human Brainwork*, Chicago, Kew & Co, 1906.
2. Jean Pierre Fourcade: *Le Point*, 24 February 1975.
3. *Le Monde*, 10–11 August 1975.
4. *Le Monde*, 11 October 1974.

3. Man and his penis

1. A. C. Kinsey: *Sexual Behaviour in the Human Female*, London, W. B. Saunders, 1953.

2. W. H. Masters and V. E. Johnson: *Human Sexual Response*, New York, Little, Brown & Co., 1966.

3. *Ibid.*

4. Bruno Bettelheim: *Symbolic Wounds*, Chicago, The Free Press, 1954.

5. *Ibid.*

6. Sigmund Freud: *Moses and Monotheism*, London, Hogarth, 1939.

7. Unsigned article: 'Etude du pénis', *Union*, no. 7, January 1973.

8. David Reuben: *Everything You Always Wanted to Know about Sex*, London and New York, W. H. Allen, 1970.

4. Man and sexuality

1. Montaigne: *Essays*, Harmondsworth, Penguin, 1970.

2. 'M': *The Sensuous Man*, London, W. H. Allen, 1971.

3. Simone de Beauvoir: *The Second Sex*, Harmondsworth, Penguin, 1972.

4. Susan Brownmiller: *Against Our Will*, New York, Simon & Schuster, 1975.

5. Letters page: *Libération*, 8 July 1976.

6. Euripides: *Helen*, Harmondsworth, Penguin, 1969.

7. Susan Brownmiller: *Against Our Will*.

8. Pierre Samuel: *Amazones, Guerrières et Gaillardes*, Brussels, Editions Complexe, 1975.

9. Bronislaw Malinowski: *The Sexual Life of Savages in N.W. Melanesia*, London, Routledge & Sons, 1932.

10. *Le Nouvel Observateur*, 8 April 1974.

5. The myth of the phallic orgasm

1. W. H. Masters and V. E. Johnson: *Human Sexual Inadequacy*, London, Churchill, 1970.

2. Christianne Rochefort: 'Le Mythe de la Frigidité Féminine', *Partisans*, nos. 54–5, July–October 1970.

3. Wilhelm Reich: *Function of the Orgasm*, London, Panther, 1968.

4. *Ibid.*

5. *Ibid.*

6. 'Apostrophes', 13 June 1975.

7. Masters and Johnson: *Human Sexual Inadequacy*.

8. David Reuben: *Everything You Always Wanted to Know about Sex*, London and New York, W. H. Allen, 1970.

9. W. H. Masters and V. E. Johnson: *Human Sexual Response*, New York, Little, Brown & Co, 1966.

10. Masters and Johnson: *Human Sexual Inadequacy*.

11. David Reuben: *Everything You Always Wanted to Know about Sex*.

6. The daddy and the rapist

1. Heidi Hartman: 'Capitalism, Patriarchy and Job Segregation by Sex', *Signs: Journal of Women in Culture and Society*, vol. 1, no. 3, spring 1976.

2. *Questions Féministes*, no. 2, February 1978.

3. Simone de Beauvoir: *The Second Sex*, Harmondsworth, Penguin, 1972.

4. Pope Paul VI: Speech on 20 October 1966.

5. *Questions Féministes*, no. 2, February 1978.

6. *Questions Féministes*, no. 3, May 1978.

7. Abraham Moles: 'Open Letter to the Situationists', *Internationale Situationiste*, no. 9, August 1964.

8. Alfred Jarry: *L'Amour Absolu*, Paris, Mercure de France, 1964.

9. F. Nietzsche: quoted in Simone de Beauvoir, *The Second Sex*.

10. Odile Dhavernas: *Droits des Femmes, Pouvoir des Hommes*, Paris, Seuil, 1978.

11. Letters page: *Libération*, 8 July 1976.

12. Emmanuèle Durand: 'Le Viol', *Partisans*, nos. 54–6, July–October 1970.

13. Collette Guillaumin: *Questions Féministes*, no. 2, February 1978.

7. Marriage

1. Odile Dhavernas: *Droits des Femmes, Pouvoir des Hommes*, Paris, Seuil, 1978.

2. *Ibid*.

3. The Hosken Report: 'Genital/Sexual Mutilation of Females', *WIN News*, November 1979.

4. *Playboy*, French edition, May 1974.

5. Report from Comité Emplois-Revenus, Documentation Française, July 1980.

6. *Questions Féministes*, nos. 2 and 3, February and May 1978.

8. Between men

1. Raoul Vaneigem; *Traité de Savoir-Vivre à l'Usage des Jeunes Générations*, Paris, Gallimard, 1967.

2. Voline: *La Révolution Inconnue*, Paris, 1972.

3. *Ibid.*

4. 'Solidaridad Obrera', *Femmes Libres*, Claix, La Pensée Sauvage, 1977.

5. *Ibid.*

6. Eldridge Cleaver: *Soul on Ice*, London, Jonathan Cape, 1969.

7. *La Proclamation de la Commune*, Paris, Gallimard, 1965.

8. Karl Marx: *Communist Manifesto*, Moscow, Progress Publishers, 1971.

9. Paul Mattick: *Krisen und Krisentheorien*, Frankfurt, Fischer-Taschenbuch-Verlag, 1974.